RSC
ROYAL SHAKESPEARE COMPANY

STRA

PROJEKT EUROPA

A SEASON CELEBRATING THE BEST OF EUROPEAN THEATRE

TICKETS ON SALE
FROM 11 NOVEMBER

RSC.ORG.UK

The work of the RSC Literary Department is generously supported by The Drue and H.J. Heinz II Charitable Trust

ARTS COUNCIL ENGLAND

GRANTA

12 Addison Avenue, London W11 4QR | email: editorial@granta.com
To subscribe go to granta.com, or call 020 8955 7011 (free phone 0500 004 033)
in the United Kingdom, 845-267-3031 (toll-free 866-438-6150) in the United States

ISSUE 149: AUTUMN 2019

PUBLISHER AND EDITOR	Sigrid Rausing
DEPUTY EDITOR	Rosalind Porter
POETRY EDITOR	Rachael Allen
DIGITAL DIRECTOR	Luke Neima
ASSISTANT EDITOR	Francisco Vilhena
SENIOR DESIGNER	Daniela Silva
DEPUTY ONLINE EDITOR	Eleanor Chandler
EDITORIAL ASSISTANT	Lucy Diver
OPERATIONS AND SUBSCRIPTIONS	Mercedes Forest
MARKETING	Aubrie Artiano, Simon Heafield
PUBLICITY	Pru Rowlandson, publicity@granta.com
CONTRACTS	Isabella Depiazzi
TO ADVERTISE CONTACT	Renata Molina Lopes, Renata.Molina-Lopes@granta.com
FINANCE	Mercedes Forest, Elizabeth Wedmore
SALES MANAGER	Katie Hayward
IT MANAGER	Mark Williams
PRODUCTION ASSOCIATE	Sarah Wasley
PROOFS	Katherine Fry, Jessica Kelly, Lesley Levene, Josie Mitchell, Jess Porter, Vimbai Shire, Martha Sprackland
CONTRIBUTING EDITORS	Daniel Alarcón, Anne Carson, Mohsin Hamid, Isabel Hilton, Michael Hofmann, A.M. Homes, Janet Malcolm, Adam Nicolson, Edmund White

This selection copyright © 2019 Granta Publications and individual contributors.

Granta, ISSN 173231 (USPS 508), is published four times a year by Granta Publications, 12 Addison Avenue, London W11 4QR, United Kingdom.

The US annual subscription price is $48. Airfreight and mailing in the USA by agent named Worldnet-Shipping USA Inc., 156-15 146th Avenue, 2nd Floor, Jamaica, NY 11434, USA. Periodicals postage paid at Jamaica, NY 11431.

US Postmaster: Send address changes to *Granta*, Worldnet-Shipping USA Inc., 156-15 146th Avenue, 2nd Floor, Jamaica, NY 11434, USA.

Subscription records are maintained at *Granta*, c/o Abacus e-Media, 21 Southampton Row, London, WC1B 5HA.

Air Business Ltd is acting as our mailing agent.

Granta is printed and bound in Italy by Legoprint. This magazine is printed on paper that fulfils the criteria for 'Paper for permanent document' according to ISO 9706 and the American Library Standard ANSI/NIZO Z39.48-1992 and has been certified by the Forest Stewardship Council (FSC). *Granta* is indexed in the American Humanities Index.

ISBN 978-1-909-889-28-6

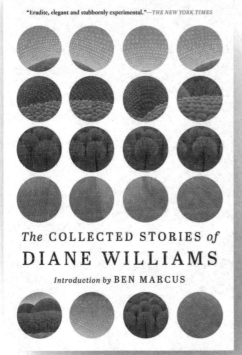

DEPARTMENT FOR
CONTINUING
EDUCATION

UNIVERSITY OF
OXFORD

Part-time courses in
Creative Writing
and Literature

Short courses:
online courses, summer schools, weekend lectures
and weekly classes

Oxford qualifications:
undergraduate awards and postgraduate degrees
Applications now open

@OxfordConted

www.conted.ox.ac.uk/granta19

The castles country houses and carrot cake in the café Pass

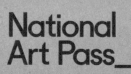

The magazine of Chatham House covering international affairs

A resource for governments, businesses and academics since 1945

Fresh thinking on the way the world is run and how to improve it

The World Today

Subscribe today and stay informed

theworldtoday.org   +44 (0)20 3544 9725

CONTENTS

Introduction

To think about Europe is to think about the thorny old issue of longing and belonging; nostalgia, homesickness, exile, migration and community. To think about Europe is to make sweeping statements, often about history and philosophy. 'No other continent', we may begin, or 'The European Enlightenment tradition', or 'Our values'. But if history and anthropology teach us anything, it is that few cultural traditions properly belong to one place – people have traded stories since time immemorial, and still do; good stories and bad, merging and re-emerging. And yet places have themes, particular melodies and phrases and rhythms that are curiously durable.

We asked a number of European writers to select, and (briefly) reflect on, a quote about Europe. We were curious about what writers like Orhan Pamuk or Ludmila Ulitskaya might choose – who would our contributors turn to when asked to think about 'Europe', and what do they make of our continent, now? Tellingly, with one exception – Marie Darrieussecq, who quoted *National Geographic* – the quotes are steeped in history. Our authors evoked the great (male) canon: Fyodor Dostoevsky, William Blake, Bertolt Brecht, Joseph Conrad, Albert Camus. The quotes speak broadly to the darkness of Europe's history, not its freedoms and affluence: 'What times are these, in which / A conversation about trees is almost a crime' (Brecht, 1939). Some are defiant – 'Our Europe is a shared adventure which we will continue to pursue, despite you, in the wind of intelligence' (Camus, *Letters to a German Friend*, 1944) – others caustic: 'Well then, eliminate the people, curtail them, force them to be silent. Because the European Enlightenment is more important than people' (Dostoevsky).

Europe's song, it seemed to me reading these pieces, is set to music of grandiosity and lament, hubris and guilt. The weight of history binds us. Even Marie Darrieussecq turns mournful in her piece. There is a Europe of death and a Europe of life, she writes. Mass graves, bloodstained snow, sublime forests, there you have it. History divides 'Europe' from 'Britain', these symbolic entities of shifting borders.

That atmosphere remains in the longer texts, too. Thus William Atkins follows in Chekhov's footsteps to the Russian island Sakhalin north of Japan, a penal colony of Imperial Russia and the Soviet Union. What is that neglected land like now? This is beyond the edge of Europe, a place whose Indigenous people, the Nivkh, have been marginalised for so long that they are nearly forgotten.

Katherine Angel writes about the attempt to decolonise a Belgian museum – the Musée royal de l'Afrique centrale. The most racist objects in the museum, including the Leopard Man (see illustration in the text), are now regarded as *hors-jeu* – out of play – and gathered in a special room. But Angel's essay is also about her ambiguous relationship with London, where she lives and works. She ends with a quote from Günther Anders, the German-Jewish philosopher. He was born Stern, but published under the name Anders, a Nordic-sounding name and also the word for 'other', or 'different', in German. Günther Stern was Walter Benjamin's cousin, and at one time Hannah Arendt's husband. He fled to France, and then the US, returning to Europe (Vienna) in 1950. 'Each of us knows that our mother is mortal, none of us knows that our home is mortal', he wrote.

The Holocaust haunts us. British cultural historian Lara Feigel describes a long-ago visit to her Belgian grandmother, a survivor of Birkenau, who had cut herself off from the family of her eldest son, Feigel's father, after he married out. Feigel reflects on an old diary entry describing the visit and the (almost) lost Jewish heritage of her family.

Joseph Leo Koerner, an eminent American art historian, travels with his children to the Nazi site of mass murder on the outskirts of Minsk in Belarus. His Viennese paternal grandparents were killed there, buried in a mass grave. Koerner explores a complex familial resistance to the painful question of what, exactly, happened to them. They were gone, deported and killed, no one knew where. He recalls childhood summers in Vienna, where his artist father compulsively painted street and landscape scenes; prolonged and unarticulated rituals of grief. The text is illustrated with one of Henry Koerner's paintings; an interior of his childhood home. A thread, a surreal element, unwinds like a spider's web from the ball of yarn on the table to the lamp above his mother's hands. The stillness of the scene, the association to cobwebs, speaks of death and loss. There is another image in the piece: a poster, dating from 1941, showing the deportation ('emigration') of Austria's Jews – other threads winding their way from Vienna to the complex of Nazi camps and killing fields.

The story of the Holocaust is also the story of failed asylum systems. We live with that legacy still. Ulf Karl Olov Nilsson, a Swedish psychoanalyst and poet, writes about his work on a psychiatric ward. A young woman from an unnamed African country has been denied asylum after a linguistic assessment cast doubt on her national origin. She is now almost catatonic. Nilsson eventually got her to speak: she revealed that she had witnessed several members of her family being killed, after which she was imprisoned in a cellar, where she was repeatedly raped. This essay, a chapter from his book *Glömskans bibliotek* (The Library of Oblivion), is concerned with the paralysed silence at the heart of trauma and the obscenity, in that context, of interrogating asylum claims on behalf of the state.

And yet of course the work of assessing, recording and interrogating acts of violence has to be done. We can't approve legal claims without due process; there is no restorative justice without investigations. Without that, we have no history and no analysis, only laments: eulogies for the dead and wounded. But interrogating trauma has to be done with compassion and respect, a delicate balancing act between emotions and facts and context. Somewhere in-between is the truth. Somewhere in-between is the story, or at least the European story.

Brexit note: I apologise in advance if this issue reaches you later than normal. We have printed *Granta* in Italy for many years now, transporting it across open borders – good luck with that, someone said. Good luck indeed.

We all know that our mother is mortal, none of us knows that our home is mortal. ∎

Sigrid Rausing

Peter Mishler

The Taste of the Feeling

Shy yet contemptible object
in an unleaking vial collected.
It slips from end to end
and back, the jaw of it
elsewhere unendingly
dreaming, its child
discarded in tactical gear.
It is the original taste,
the taste of the feeling,
as end to end and back
and forth it slips, it waves
to its relevant world
full of filth and wellness
and poisons and grit
and laughter at pics
of the unwashed shopping,
of heated plastics
and mood-based buying,
redeemers-in-headsets,
and children in tactical gear.
An unleaking thing in a vial
collected. Then strung
from a hook. Then lowered
to clamps. Then held
in its place in the depths,
and shaken, and drunk.

My Parents I, 1944
Courtesy of the artist's estate

MALY TROSTINETS

Joseph Leo Koerner

The trip was my son's idea. Leo's spring break no longer overlapped with his younger sister's, and she would be going to Colonial Williamsburg, to fit her grade's focus on early America, then on to Barbados. He wanted something equal but opposite. At school there had been debates about affinity groups, about who qualified for one and whose identity needed support now, in the Trump era. Leo got caught up in a dispute about whether the internment of Japanese Americans in the Second World War was worse than the Nazis' treatment of the Jews. Perhaps because Holocaust history wasn't on the curriculum, or maybe just because of who joined the debate, the consensus seemed to him to lean toward Japanese–American internment as the greater injustice. Arguments around victimhood, reading *Man is Wolf to Man* – Janusz Bardach's memoir of the Gulag – and a sibling's impulse to counter Caribbean travel with something cold and rainy, all steered him toward a journey I had several times planned but never undertaken, to Minsk in Belarus.

For five years I had been making a documentary about Vienna. Half the film chronicled the Viennese invention of the modern architecture of home. I explored dreams of homemaking dreamed by the city's leading architects, artists and thinkers – Klimt, Adolf Loos, Freud, Wittgenstein, etc. – as they tried to make the expanding capital of the Habsburg Empire livable for ethnically diverse and mutually antagonistic immigrants. The other half was personal. It revolved around a painting by my father depicting the living room of his childhood home in Vienna, with his parents, Leo and Fanny Körner, safe inside. My father had escaped Austria in 1938, leaving his parents behind. He created the painting from memory in 1944 in Washington DC, while waiting to be shipped to Europe as an officer in the information branch of the US Army. It came to hang above my childhood bed in Pittsburgh, Pennsylvania, where my father met my mother and settled in 1952. What fascinated me about the work was less its meticulous inventory of my grandparents' vanished home than a strange coincidence that occurred in it. Through a window in the depicted living room, at the far end of a vertiginous street view my father managed almost photographically to recollect, there appeared, tiny but recognizable through their distinctive semicircular entablatures, the two windows of our own top-floor apartment in Vienna, where we spent our summers. Back in 1944, when my father reimagined them, our apartment's windows belonged to a kind of pictorial shorthand for other people's homes. One long block of anonymous apartment buildings, each facade featuring scores of nearly, but never quite identical windows, ours happen to occur in the painting almost at its perspectival vanishing point – what in German is called the *Fluchtpunkt*, which means, literally, the point of flight or escape. By 1968, when we began to lease our two-room flat on the Volkertplatz, at the end of the street leading back to my father's old home, no one realized that he had perfectly but inadvertently captured our telltale windows in his painting. To me, who first noticed the detail, the imaginary bridge spanning the two homes seemed uncanny.

In the film, my father's painting starts as just one expression of the dream of the Viennese interior. It illustrates how ordinary people turned their small rented flats (everyone rents in Vienna) into beautiful enclaves. But exploring the later history of the apartment – how my grandparents were evicted to make room for 'Aryan' tenants, and how their neighbor in the apartment right next door, a fervent Nazi who claimed to have personally founded the Hitler Movement in Austria, seized the whole apartment building from its Jewish owners – the story veers to nightmare. Overnight, after Hitler's 12 March 1938 annexation of Austria, Vienna's 200,000 Jews effectively lost their right to live in the city. In the film the story of the Körners and their apartment is told by an archivist from the Israelitische Kultusgemeinde Wien (Vienna Israelite Community). The Kultusgemeinde is where, since 1849, births and deaths of Vienna's Jews are recorded. After 1938, the institution was forced to organize the emigration and deportation of Jews. For Fanny and Leo the paper trail turned out to be chillingly complete. Not only their forced 'deregistration' to Minsk, but also the precise facts of their transport there by train were fully documented. Commanded to report to a 'collection point' in the Sperlgasse for 'resettlement' in the German-occupied East, they departed in the early hours of 9 June 1942 from Vienna's Aspang railway station aboard a special train with the designation Da 206 (the 'Da' stood for David, as in Star of David). At Vawkavysk, formerly Wołkowysk, the track gauge changed and passengers were forced from third-class cars into cattle cars – police reports record deaths already here.

Even with his excellent Czech, Polish, Belarus and Russian, our archivist struggled to read aloud the stations listed on the twisting route from Vienna to Minsk, since some of the towns had disappeared, their names forgotten or changed. Caught on film, his halting reading of these names from the original train report helped conjure the distance traversed. Further documentation revealed that in Minsk the 1,006 passengers of Da 206 were herded into trucks and driven twelve kilometers southeast to a place called Maly Trostinets. There on the afternoon of 15 June, within a stand of young pine trees deep in the Blagovshchina Forest, they were shot, their bodies then thrown into long ditches and covered with quicklime. Later transports arrived at Maly Trostinets by train along tracks that had been previously abandoned, and gas vans replaced murder by shooting, but the protocol – execution immediately upon arrival in the early afternoon – and the place in the forest remained the same.

Maly Trostinets, camp entrance, c.1944
Courtesy of the United States Holocaust Memorial Museum

My son had helped with sound in an early interview for the film, and he had heard talk of a reconnaissance trip to Minsk and Maly Trostinets. In the end we decided to confine the filming to Vienna, letting the archivist's voice gesture toward the unimaginable. But our failure to follow through on our plans bothered Leo. Reading up on the twentieth-century history of Belarus where, after starvation and mass killings already under Stalin's rule, the Nazi occupiers killed about a third of the total population, including some 250,000 Jews, and where, since 1994, people still live under Soviet-style dictator Alexander Lukashenko, Leo proposed a journey by train from Vienna via Warsaw and Vawkavysk to Minsk. There we would stay in the gigantic Hotel Belarus, with its panoramic views of the city and an enormous swimming pool decorated with social-realist

mosaics of athletes, Red Army liberators and muscular Viking Rus'.
To orient ourselves we would visit the Museum of Architectural
Miniatures, where most of Belarus's monuments and castles can be
visually explored in tiny scale models. Using Yandex.Taxi, the app
which Leo promised to obtain, we would be driven out to the Mound
of Glory, a pair of soaring bayonet-shaped obelisks atop a huge hill
formed of scorched soil from the country's 'heroic' destroyed cities,
much of the soil carried by hand by schoolchildren. Time permitting
we would spend an afternoon at the Stalin Line Museum. There a
segment of the fortifications that ran along the erstwhile western
border of the Soviet Union (built to withstand a Polish invasion but
useless against the Germans in 1941) has been carefully restored,
and vintage mortars and Kalashnikov rifles can be fired for a modest
fee. Maly Trostinets itself, online comments report, could be reached
only with difficulty by bus, and taxi drivers could not be expected
to have heard of the place. The sprawling Memorial Complex was
also said to be confusing, with monuments and plaques containing
inaccurate or contradictory information. But Leo downloaded a
whole library of maps and made certain that Minsk was a safe place
even for tourists who had lost their way. His proposal was hard to
turn down, since I had a week free in March, and his half-siblings,
Ben and Sigi, were eager to join us from England. I also secretly
regretted my own peculiar inertia, which had paralyzed me as far
back as I can remember.

The fate of my father's parents had always been the great family
mystery. The Nazis had murdered almost all his relatives: this
was all we knew and all we thought could be known. Two younger
cousins managed to escape via child transports to England and
Palestine, and they learned nothing more than that all the ones
unknown to us, the ones living in Vienna as well as the oil-mining
relatives in Boryslav and Stryi, in Galicia, now western Ukraine, had
vanished without a trace. In the absence of facts, rumors flourished. In
1941 my father's brother Kurt had been deported with his wife Olga to

Kielce, in occupied Poland, and a letter to my father from his parents in Vienna seemed to suggest that they contemplated joining Kurt. This would have meant that they, together with Kurt and Olga, would have probably died in Treblinka after the liquidation of the Kielce ghetto in August 1942. Other concentration camps were sometimes named. A college course on the anthropology of kinship required from each student a family tree. I listed eighteen of the disappeared relatives on my father's side as having died in Auschwitz, followed by a question mark. On the other hand, I dimly remembered having once been shown a note with the words '*abgemeldet nach Minsk*' written on it in my mother's hand. *Abgemeldet* (deregistered) was correctly spelled, so I assumed that my mother, who barely spoke German, must have transcribed the word from somewhere, or had it spelled out to her, but her recollection of where she got this information was cloudy and her theory about it – that her parents-in-law might have fled eastward into Russia – caused me to ignore the clue.

The idea that Leo and Fanny somehow survived obsessed my mother. For years she read nothing but Holocaust literature and collected newspaper stories about lost relatives turning up out of nowhere. She disliked her own parents up in Escanaba, especially her father, whose Catholic piety concealed a violent temperament. And she had little in common with her sister's family in Iowa – all incurious Lutherans who never once left the US. An aspiring concert violinist on a scholarship to a music conservatory in Pittsburgh, she met and married my father. Divorced, exotic and seventeen years her senior, my father was partly an escape from her own family. She identified with my father's family and contemplated converting to Judaism even though my father's parents had abandoned that faith. She felt closest to his mother, Fanny, who was supposed to have been independent, sensible and strong – as opposed to the supposedly passive, emotionally frozen Leo. She imagined Fanny still alive, alone and trapped in Siberia or China. My father did little to counter this fantasy. He would just shake his head in annoyance and mutter to my sister and me that this was 'a bunch of shit', while my mother held up her theory as yet more proof of his callousness. 'Your father only thinks about himself.'

What exactly he knew remains to me a mystery, but that he knew that they were murdered was obvious. Reading through old letters, I found that already in 1946 my father had enquired at the Red Cross in Vienna and confirmed that his parents were dead. Furloughed from the army, he had also visited a close Christian family friend, an unmarried secretary at the national railway, who passed on to him some vital papers concerning his two surviving cousins. By the time I met her, Stefanie Lukas had become a deeply unpleasant old lady who forced us to call her 'Aunt Steffi' and whose apartment was crammed full of valuables originally belonging to my grandparents – we would have coffee and cakes with her seated around a table covered with a beautiful lace doily made by my grandmother's hand. These things were probably given to her for temporary safekeeping, but she never admitted it, and at her death, out of spite, she left everything to her cleaning lady who (we think) kept the good things and threw everything else away. Having boarded for a time in my father's family home, Aunt Steffi knew all about Leo and Fanny's eviction, their reduced accommodation in two successive Jewish 'collective apartments' and their deportation to the East. She could have given a full account of their final days in Vienna, but she chose not to. Instead she spoke to us endlessly about her own plight during the war, and how, dressed in her office uniform, she stayed for days in one of the huge bunkers in the Augarten as the bombs destroyed the buildings all around.

In the army my father had served in the OSS, the Office of Strategic Service, the wartime predecessor of the CIA. He designed posters and brochures that publicized information on the enemy, including Nazi atrocities. After his discharge in April 1946, he re-enlisted in the US military government in Germany, so throughout the war and afterwards he had early access to facts about the Holocaust. The paintings he made in Berlin at the time, which established his international reputation, were explicit acknowledgments of, and monuments to, the murder of his parents. It was obvious to us as children that our yearly four-month stays in Vienna, made ostensibly so that my father could paint from life views of the city and its environs, were in fact a protracted form of mourning. Why else would we, each year, leave our happy life in Pittsburgh to travel to what seemed to us a ghost town in order to trail after my father while he looked for things to paint? And why else would we end up of all places there, on the Volkertplatz, in an apartment whose only selling point was its view? For me the painting of my grandparents in their living room came to symbolize this unquiet past. It must have been painted when my father had some hope that they were still alive. On the table between them, he shows the esoteric board game – an invention by his hobbyist father – still in play, with the blues and yellows almost tied. And he lets the string from his mother's knitting rise up over the blown-glass arms of the chandelier and down to the little dancing ball of thread as if to connect himself and us viewers back to home, to the mother who, Penelope-like, weaves as she awaits the exiled hero's return. And in fact, on forms filled out for his military service in 1944, when he painted that looping thread, he still listed his mother as his closest living relative. Via the painting's glimpse of the Volkertplatz, then, the painting also managed continually to project this tiny but real glimmer of hope forward into the future, into our home that we therefore restlessly inhabited.

It wasn't until 1997 that I discovered the facts. I was in Vienna writing the catalogue for a retrospective of my father's work at the Belvedere. Knowing how reluctant the Viennese audience was about confronting its Nazi past, I felt queasy about my incurious vagueness concerning my grandparents' deaths. 'Auschwitz' with a question mark felt woefully inadequate in such a context. Through a friend visiting from Oxford I chanced to meet Simon Wiesenthal, who told me to go to the 'Bevölkerungsamt' – he spoke the word slowly so I could write it down – but no institution by that name was to be found. Then, in the process of paying my German translator, I visited the

offices of *Illustrierte Neue Welt*, a Jewish journal founded in 1897 by
Theodor Herzl and still published in Vienna. There the editor-in-
chief (my translator's mother) told me what to do. You simply went to
the Israelitische Kultusgemeinde and they would tell you everything
there was to know. Later that day I found myself across the desk from
the duty archivist in her windowless office adjacent to Vienna's main
synagogue. Before I could finish describing my mission, Frau Weiss
reached for a big book of birth records and brusquely opened it to
the right page: 'Heinrich Sieghart Körner, born Vienna, August 28,
1915, died St Pölten July 4, 1991.' It was less my father's name, with
its original, long-abandoned Wagnerian 'Sieghart', that took me by
surprise than the precision concerning his recent death, because the
archive felt so much like a time capsule, with old records preserved
but no longer updated. While I mumbled something appreciative,
Frau Weiss – on the basis of my father's birth record – had swiftly
located a slip of yellowed paper in a big cardboard box, which she laid
neatly before me. There, written in ink in one script, was the name
'Leo Körner', and the words '*mit Gattin nach Minsk*'. A note had
been added in another script in pencil '*(deportiert)*'. Remembering
my mother's mysterious note, I believed I stood again before the
same impasse. But Frau Weiss, assuming a practiced bedside manner,
explained that all of the more than 9,000 Viennese Jews officially
deregistered to Minsk had in fact been forcibly deported – the word
'deported' on the yellowed slip had been added after 1945, probably
by an archivist like Frau Weiss. And all these many thousands had
only passed through Minsk, through back tracks in its freight train
station, sent secretly on their way to a terrible place called Maly
Trostinets. There they were all shot or gassed upon arrival. We know
this, she explained, because of train records, war trials testimony
and a single survivor's report – only seventeen people were known
to have survived transports from the German Reich 'to Minsk'.

Frau Weiss then showed me an old handmade poster on her office
wall diagramming the bureaucratic maze devised to make leaving
Austria first difficult and expensive for the Jews and then impossible,

as emigration turned into forced transport to death camps in the East. Created by someone employed in the Israelitische Kultusgemeinde Wien, the poster resembled Otto Neurath's utopian Isotypes, but put to murderous use – its creator was probably killed in 1942.

Frau Weiss also gave me pamphlets to read. I learned that the use of Maly Trostinets as a killing site marked an important turning point in the Nazi genocide. Hitler intended his invasion of the Soviet Union to be a swift war of extinction. Not only was the Bolshevik enemy to be destroyed, entire populations were to be killed or starved to death to create *Lebensraum* for Germany. German and 'Germanic' colonizers would farm what would become the vast new breadbasket of his Thousand-Year Reich. By late 1941, Hitler steered these murderous plans more urgently toward the Jews. The masses of Jewish people in the conquered territories, together with the remaining Jews of Germany and Austria, would be transported by train to purpose-built killing factories. Unlike concentration camps, which killed some prisoners and worked others to death, these camps would exterminate new arrivals immediately, using poison gas, and their remains would be incinerated in huge crematoria. The few prisoners forced to do the gassing and burning would also be killed in efficient rotation, leaving no witnesses or evidence behind. Such operations would be undertaken in territories far to the east of the German Reich. Shrouded in the fog of war and soaked with the blood of Stalin's atrocities, the lands around Minsk seemed optimum for this purpose. A railway hub, Minsk had long-distance tracks in all directions, as well as spur lines to obscure enclaves close by. One of these was the abandoned Soviet kolkhoz 'Karl Marx' beside the village of Maly Trostinets – the name means 'Little Trostinets' and has many alternative spellings: Trostenets, Trostinez, Trascianiec, Trostenec, Trastsianiets, Tras'tsanyets. With tracks leading into it, buildings sufficient to house guards and slave workers, and two secluded forests at its edge, this tiny settlement – emptied of its inhabitants and fenced as an off-limits *Wehrdorf* – became an improvised forerunner of the huge extermination camps under construction in occupied Poland,

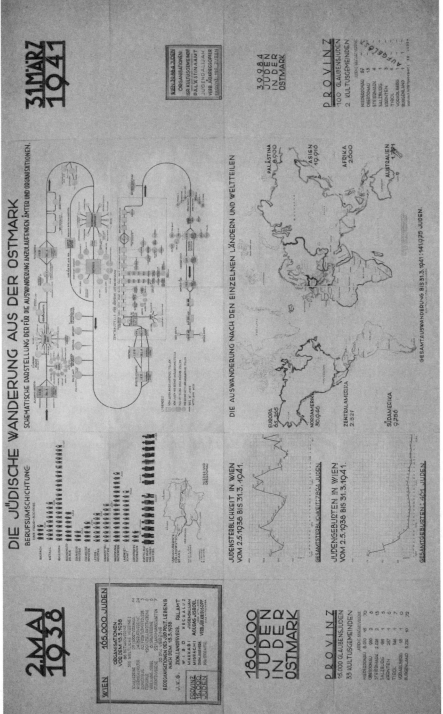

The *Jewish Emigration from Ostmark* (Austria), hand-drawn wall roster on twenty sheets, 1941
Courtesy of the Israelitische Kultusgemeinde Wien

something between a killing site like Babi Yar and the industrial death facilities of Treblinka, Sobibor and Belzec.

The Jews of Vienna were the first in the German Reich to be deported for 'resettlement' in the East. This little-known distinction was the direct consequence of another forgotten Austrian first, the eviction of Jews from their homes in 1938. It was Vienna's grassroots anti-Semitism that invented, suddenly and to the surprise of the Nazi authorities, the idea of rendering Jewish citizens homeless and at the mercy of the police. It was also mainly Viennese Jews who, between 6 May and 10 October 1942, were murdered in Maly Trostinets. Tens of thousands of Jews from elsewhere died there too, together with Soviet soldiers, Belarusian citizens, both Jewish and Christian, and partisans. The total estimated death count ranges from 80,000 to more than 300,000; the signage at the Memorial Complex claims 206,000, on the basis of an early Soviet report. After the Nazi defeat at Smolensk in October 1943, a massive secret exhumation action was launched to hide the killings from the approaching Red Army. Soviet prisoners were forced to reopen the ditches in the Blagovshchina Forest and carry the decomposed corpses – called *figuren* (figures) by the Nazi commander Arthur Harder – to a colossal bonfire, fueled by wood gathered forcibly from neighboring farmers. The unearthed remains were sifted for dental gold and burned in five-meter-high piles on a grill constructed of train rails.

Maly Trostinets's existence was uncovered when the Red Army retook Minsk in July 1944 and found at its outskirts thirty-four huge smoldering pits filled with ashes, twisted tracks and human remains. After 1945 the area was forgotten, a fenced-off no man's land. Parts became landfill – mushroom-shaped methane vents still stud the fields around the memorials, and in the 1990s, fragments of toppled Soviet-era monuments were dumped on the wasteland while new apartment blocks rose up all around. The history of Maly Trostinets was further obscured by the sheer number of killing sites in Belarus. During their three-year occupation, the Nazis destroyed, by some estimates, as many as 5,000 villages and 600 towns, killing most or all of the inhabitants, and operated at least seventy death camps. The Soviet authorities sealed the archives, since vast numbers of Belarusians had been murdered by Stalin's secret police between 1938 and 1941, and in 1989 a Belarus commission indicated that at least 30,000 people perished in the woods of Kurapaty, just a few kilometers from Blagovshchina Forest. The place name Maly Trostinets itself disappeared from maps when the area became incorporated into greater Minsk. Until the 1990s, when the archives were opened up to historians, the enigma of my grandparents' disappearance was a collective mystery shared by thousands of families with Viennese relatives.

We arrived in Minsk at an auspicious moment. In five days' time, just after our departure, President Alexander Lukashenko together with Chancellor Sebastian Kurz of Austria and a host of dignitaries would inaugurate the first monument at Maly Trostinets to openly acknowledge the murder of Viennese Jews. Vladimir, our guide and a filmmaker who had just completed a documentary about the Minsk ghetto, had announced our visit to the Austrian ambassador to Belarus, as well as to Belarus state television, turning our visit into a minor public event. Vladimir's daughter, an aspiring documentarian herself, filmed us together with the TV crew, as if to create a 'making of' film of the network coverage. In reality, she just hoped to put together a film for our family, while the television crew itself was just shooting B-roll for their coverage of the official ceremony. Rain was predicted for that day and interviews with survivors' families would be harder to organize.

As a child I was troubled by having two persons in my head. One was an 'I' that lurked in silence deep inside me. The other was a voice, loud and vociferous, that narrated, usually mockingly, whatever it saw me doing. This 'announcer', as I called it, couldn't be shut up, and if ever the inaudible 'I' managed to conjure a third person to speak on its behalf, the 'announcer' would only shout louder his rude commentary. Over time these struggles ebbed, perhaps because the 'announcer' finally became me. But Maly Trostinets somehow brought the two inner persons back to mind as I tried to edit out from my experience the various people documenting it, myself included. On the way to the Blagovshchina killing site, walking through five stylized train carriages intended to symbolize the last journey taken by victims before their death, Vladimir invited me to imagine my grandparents there. Speaking softly into my ear, he recalled what is known about those final moments, how the arrivals had to leave their labeled suitcases in a neat pile for later delivery, how they were fooled into thinking they had reached their promised new homes, and how, in groups small enough to control, they were forced to undress and kneel at the edge of the pit. I knew these details, all of them extracted from war trials testimony and a single witness report, and I would have wanted to walk the choreographed path by myself, or hand in hand with my children. But of course I could have done that as well, instead, and I was grateful to Vladimir for his effort, as I knew from long before that such imaginings were completely beyond me, and it now seemed indecent to my grandparents' memory for me to picture them doing that here, in this real place where I walked.

On scores of trees in the forest, people had hung yellow laminated memorial plaques with the first names and death dates of murdered relatives. My children wandered under the tall pine trees looking for the names Fanny and Leo, to no avail. In the forest the TV crew turned their camera away; Vladimir stood quietly in the wings. I had the feeling of being, literally, too close to the trees to see the forest. The only past that came back to me was the one my father recollected most vividly: his parents, strolling in their beloved Vienna Woods.

The common German word for monument is *denkmal*, from *denken* (to think) and *mal* (to mark or to sign). Monuments are marks, sheer presences of one kind or another, that cause one to think, perhaps in a state of reproof – a German synonym for *denkmal* is *mahnmal*, from *mahnen* (to warn or to admonish). The word *mal* has a temporal charge and can also mean a point in time or an event, as in *diesmal* (this time) or *es war einmal* (once upon a time), and indeed most monuments are there to make us think about the past. The more historically conscious a culture, the more monuments it builds. In the nineteenth century, Germany was the veritable homeland of historical consciousness. There history came to be understood as the principal force and secret 'cunning' of human life. By a strange twist of irony, what the Germans did in the twentieth century precipitated the greatest dilemma in the history of monument-making: how to commemorate the Holocaust. Not only was there the problem that victors tend to erect monuments, and Germany was a defeated perpetrator; the cruelty and the scale of what had to be commemorated defied thought, while all traditional statements of warning, even the simple admonishment 'to remember', sound pedantic, as if made with the obscene presumption that such atrocities can ever be morally or historically understood.

In 2015, two tall bronze slabs formed of expressionistically rendered prisoners, fences and barbed wire, and representing prison camp gates set ajar, were erected at the newly landscaped Memorial Complex at Maly Trostinets. Called the Gates of Memory, the monument came with a text that spoke only of the 'Minsk residents' and 'civilians deported from Europe' who were murdered here. The familiar (and politically charged) omission of Jews as victims troubled many visitors to the site. One such visitor was Waltraud Barton. Born Protestant in Vienna, she had discovered that her paternal grandfather had divorced his first wife (a convert from Judaism) in 1938, and that, after serving as maid and nurse in the household of her now-remarried husband, she was sent to her death at Maly Trostinets. When Barton went to Maly Trostinets in 2010 to pay her respects to this forgotten family member, she was appalled to find no mention of Austrian Jewish victims and so she resolved to commemorate them, first unofficially through those yellow plaques, which she had organized, and then in the form of a permanent memorial, which eventually the Austrian government funded.

This was the monument about to be inaugurated when we made our visit, and our reactions to it were what Belarus television wanted to capture on film. Designed by the Viennese architect Daniel Sanwald and fabricated by the same Minsk sculptor who created the Gates of Memory, the new Massif of Names consists of ten closely packed columns cast from a clay model in dark gray fiber-reinforced concrete. Each pillar represents one of the train transports from Vienna, but the whole massif reads as a single fissured block, suggesting the compacted burial of bodies underneath. Its shape, dimensions, medium and avoidance of figuration recall Rachel Whiteread's Holocaust memorial on the Judenplatz in Vienna, though Sanwald's underlying idea is simpler than Whiteread's. About halfway up all the pillars, in what looks from afar like erosion or damage, runs a concave frieze of first names. When we arrived at the monument, the film crew trained its cameras on the four of us circling the massif in search of the names of my grandparents. They turned out to be widely separated, but then, as we knew without saying, theirs were common Viennese names and could stand for any number of victims of that name. Vladimir encouraged us to put pebbles on the little platforms created by their names, according to Jewish graveyard custom. His daughter had two candles at hand, which my children lit in Leo and Fanny Körner's honor.

But there was a nagging question. Since nearly all of the Viennese Jews killed at Maly Trostinets are known quite precisely by their full names and addresses, because the transport lists recorded these, why represent only first names? Why this insistence on anonymity when one powerful feature about this site is the fact that it contains such documented individuals? Austrians targeted their own meticulously registered and deregistered Jewish neighbors, and Austrians – railroad engineers, boilermen, train conductors, brakemen, stationmasters and policemen – participated knowingly in the killing, even vying with one another in their zeal, although one report survives of Viennese guards aboard the transport trains complaining of not having enough provisions for themselves, and of having to work on Sundays. An early transport was placed on a siding, with the Jews locked inside, while the Austrian train crew took Sunday off.

It turns out that it was the Belarus government that would not accept last names on the new monument. It was argued that such elaborate naming would dishonor the tens of thousands of Christian Belarusians murdered at Maly Trostinets whose names have disappeared. An old saying comes to mind: some people will never forgive the Jews for Auschwitz. Or as Thomas Hobbes put it, harm so grievous that it cannot be expiated 'inclines the doer to hate the sufferer'. What made the Nazis so punctilious as murderers was that their final solution demanded every Jew be eradicated, as one stamps out every last virus of a deadly disease. Yet even though it was this distinctive murderous hatred that preserved for posterity the names of exterminated Jews, such distinction has bred a paradoxical second-order enmity. In the minds of some in Belarus, both the Nazi perpetrators and their special enemy belong to the long list of intruders. From this perspective, the first-names-only compromise is perhaps an effort to 'decolonize' the nation's history. Rendering the Jewish dead anonymous equalizes historical representation that – so the thinking goes – has been monopolized by Jews.

I had been back in the States for about a week when I received from Vladimir a link to the official news report on the dedication ceremony. Broadcast on the All National Television, it began with an anchorman explaining that while Austria refused to remember a certain 'page of its history', President Lukashenko bravely called on all nations to create a monument 'to the Austrian citizens of Jewish origin' who died in Maly Trostinets. And suddenly there we were on film, searching the Massif of Names for Fanny and Leo. The camera had captured us artfully. Peeking around the monument's edge, or finding us through its fissures, it made our movements look candid and private: a hand placing a pebble between the L and E of 'Leo', Leo my son lighting a candle for his namesake, the four of us huddled in silence in the cold March wind. And then, intercut with these shots, there was me speaking into the microphone about family history. That interview had made Leo uneasy. He worried about how things caught on other people's cameras can come back to haunt you, although when his friends started forwarding the link he didn't seem worried.

On the deeper question of whether it would have been better to have visited Minsk on our own, he was of two minds. The television crew had been distracting, and Vladimir had turned my attention away from the family and hijacked what Leo had intended as an intimate adventure. But he and his half-brother Ben had managed to sneak off to the GUM department store, torpedoing Vladimir's 'special bus tour' of Minsk, and we avoided a curatorial tour of a School of Paris exhibition and instead walked the length of the city by ourselves to one of Leo's planned destinations: a graveyard of Soviet-era statues, with huge heads of Stalin in plaster, stone and bronze balanced on cheap storage racks. But these outings felt like stolen moments. Sigi had arrived from the airport in the middle of a dinner at a gallery restaurant with no explanation of why we were there, and because our time was so densely scheduled, it wasn't until the third day of our visit that she fully understood who Vladimir was and why he was in control. But she, Ben and Leo agreed that, on balance, our visit had been much richer thanks to our Belarus guides.

For me privacy had never really been an option. I contacted Waltraud Barton ostensibly to put us in safe hands which she did, through Vladimir, but I did so also to manage my encounter with Maly Trostinets through the buffer of outsiders. The trip felt to me like the coda to a film and not like the end of a journey, which is why it came as no surprise to find cameras on our arrival. My own film had been designed to avoid closure, since closure was impossible to achieve. Everything headed in the direction of my father's childhood home, the place pictured in his painting, yet that home, indeed the whole apartment building, had been destroyed by a firebomb – in 1946 my father took a snapshot of its ruins and labeled the photo 'My House'. Everyone working on the film agreed that the building that rose up from the rubble should not be shown, just as we, when we lived in that neighborhood, never looked up to those modern third-story windows that seemed like cruel impostors. Unable to bring closure, the film – or was it me, under the film's control? – tried nightmarishly to repeat. It took its loving shots of 'beautiful Vienna' directly from paintings by my father, and it staged the interviews with archivists and historians as curious vignettes, like the ones my father painted in the city, with me and my sister posing as models.

I hated to pose for my father. Interrupting our free movement through the city, forcing me to stand still in strange positions for hours at a time, posing exposed me to my condition as an actor in someone else's plot. And it confirmed the sense I had of myself as being always already narrated by that infernal 'announcer' to a silent audience of one. If I made peace with that inner demon it was only by putting myself in his position and telling the story of his story. The terms of that truce came back to me in Maly Trostinets. Approaching the pine forest with Vladimir's voice in my ear, I found no one at home inside me to feel what I ought to have felt. Perhaps my children, who walked before me into the woods, were able to put the past to rest, but I cannot and will not speak for them. ■

'One travels by intensity; displacements and spatial figures depend on intensive thresholds of nomadic deterritorialization . . . that simultaneously define complementary, sedentary reterritorializations.'
– Gilles Deleuze and Félix Guattari, *A Thousand Plateaus: Capitalism and Schizophrenia*, 1980, translated from the French by Brian Massumi

Europe is a construct. Far from being the natural self-expression of some 'soul' or 'spirit', it is (as Deleuze might put it) an assemblage, formed through centuries of cultural contingency, of transposition, disassembly, reconfiguration, upgrade; an invention that's constructed in *longue durée*, that is still under construction, specs and settings all negotiable. Like theatre itself, Europe is a contraption, a machine. Or, to use a term close to my writer's heart, a fiction – one of the richest, most brilliant and most dark, most full of danger and potential that has ever been composed. We reside within the European *polis*, take part in its project – which, being the project of the *polis*, is always and ineluctably political – to the extent that we accept this fiction, and accept it as a fiction; not, in a deluded way, as some essential 'truth', but rather in the manner of a script, a set of stage directions within which to operate. This process, being contingent and untied to any single tribe, locale or language – indeed, on the contrary, being borne of mass migrations and translations, of inclusions and expropriations – is absolutely unconnected to questions of blood or race. *Polis* not *ethnos*: that's the basic operating code underpinning European democracy. When those instructions are jammed into reverse, the code runs backwards, *ethnos* placed before and over *polis*, then that other European mode, or script, or fiction – fascism – grinds and jolts its way into action. *Polis* or *ethnos*; democracy or fascism. We – readers, actors, spectators, citizens – are the operators; we get to choose the script, which way to throw the switch.

Europe, right now, is sick – in theatre – and at war, in theatre, with itself. In terms of grid, of system, it's short-circuiting, suffering power cuts. It needs a meaning-generator, a machine to reanimate its scripts, codes and directions, reframe its dramatic possibilities. The bureaucrats may still be staffing the administrative building, but that's meaningless without the Dionysian enclave on the lower hillside. The Acropolis needs its theatre back. ■

This is an excerpt from a speech, entitled 'Machine for a European Theatre: a Manifesto', delivered at Berlin's Literaturhaus on 5 May 2019.

© BENJAMIN BROLET
Papaoutai, 2013

OUR HOME IS MORTAL TOO

Katherine Angel

On a Sunday chat show called *Vivement dimanche*, a staple of
French television since the late 1990s, Belgian-Rwandan singer
Stromae drifts and staggers onstage. He's performing 'Formidable', a
song of regret and disappointment – disappointment funnelled into
aggression aimed at the happiness and hopes of passers-by. He makes
an unnervingly convincing show of drunkenness: the aimlessness
punctuated by sudden jerky purpose; the precarious centre of gravity;
the grand, wobbling gestures; the slightly rolling eyes.

He stumbles down the stage steps, into the studio audience, and
fixes on the two men watching from the sofas: Michel Drucker, the
show's long-time presenter, and his guest, the French-Algerian actor
Dany Boon. Zeroing in on them, just as an agitated drunk latches on
to whoever swims into view, he addresses the song to them, mocking
their optimism, their luck, and reminding them of the truth: that love
dies, that life is suffering.

He lunges over to sit down next to Drucker, who shifts slightly
in his seat, alarmed. Dany Boon, on the other hand, is mouthing the
words of the song, tears in his eyes. Speaking his lessons of pessimism
to the men at his side, Stromae then registers the audience – and
stands up, defiant but unsteady on his feet. He reproaches them for
staring at him like he's a monkey – *Et qu'est-ce que vous avez tous à*

m'regarder comme un singe, bande de macaques vous – 'you bunch of apes, you' – and mocks them for what he takes to be their pose of saintliness. He's distressed, his face contorted, on the verge of tears – his voice a grainy, growling howl. The song ends with a strangulated whoop and a disintegration; he falls back onto the sofa, weeping.

It's painful to watch. There's a lull. Stromae composes himself; the audience is on its feet; there's a standing ovation. Stromae is a huge star in Europe, though he is far less well known in the UK. His music bounces with the insistent drive of house music, but is woven through with French chanson (there are endless comparisons to Jacques Brel in the press), American hip-hop, Cape Verdean morna and Congolese rumba. He is a formidable and unusual dancer; he hints towards breakdancing and body-popping, but doesn't fully inhabit these; his dancing is more strange and idiosyncratic. It feels informed by the mime tradition of Marcel Marceau – for instance, in the video for 'Papaoutai', a song about fathers, Stromae is an eerie, doll-like figure, an immobile, wooden stand-in for a real-life, flesh-and-blood father. A young boy dances inventively, in frustration, in front of this ersatz father, and eventually, in resignation, also takes on his rigid, wide-eyed stance. When performing the song live, Stromae begins in this mannequin pose (sometimes he gets carried onstage in this stance), later moving into his jerky yet controlled, warped robotic dancing – with grimaces, uncomfortable contortions, a strange painful twisting of himself.

The comparisons to Brel are not wrong. Like Brel's, Stromae's songs are often an intoxicating mix of absurdity and tragedy, of play and mourning. And like Brel he uses his entire self – every inch of his body, every joint, muscle, facial expression – to inhabit the song. Tiny details speak volumes. In live versions of 'Papaoutai', Stromae ornaments his vocal line, tapping into the intricate wavering of Algerian rai, the music that became a vehicle for political protest in French-colonised Algeria.

Algerian singers Rachid Taha and Khaled have had huge success in Europe, as has Turkish singer Tarkan; his 1997 hit 'Şımarık' featured in Claire Denis's 1999 film *Beau Travail*, an exploration of the erotics of colonial power, through a depiction of the French Foreign Legion's presence in Djibouti. Rachid Taha's music was deeply infused with rai, and chaabi, popular folk music. But he mixed these up with pop and rock, singing in both Arabic and French. With his band Carte de Séjour ('green card' or 'residence permit'), in 1987 he covered legendary French crooner Charles Trenet's 'Douce France', a tribute to a picture-postcard, deeply French France, with its villages and its church bells, its meadows and its rivers. This annoyed a lot of people – what was an Arab doing singing this treasure of Frenchness? – and the song was banned from some radio stations. The band's records were not sold in shops reluctant to have Arabs as customers. The mingling of genres in the work of these musicians reveals the traces of colonial power, while simultaneously talking back to that power in an assertion of hybridity, of history's material legacy.

When I was growing up in Brussels, where I was born after my father got a teaching job there in 1976, we would sometimes take the trams – wheezing and whistling through the streets – right out of town to Tervuren, a leafy, grand suburb. The number 81 would trundle from Ixelles where we lived, an area both shabby and elegant, through Montgomery, a monumental, portentous part of the city dominated by the Cinquantenaire, a park built by Leopold II in the 1880s to mark the fiftieth anniversary of the revolutions that led to the creation of Belgium. The museums in the Cinquantenaire were to bring together and exhibit the nation's knowledge, and were a crucial component of the 1897 International Exposition. Knowledge of Africa was displayed in the Palace of the Colonies, located further out in Tervuren. The palace was designed to exhibit the riches of the Free State of the Congo, as it was then known, despite being in fact the personal property of Leopold II until 1908, after which it became a Belgian colony. A 'human zoo' graced the Palace during the Exposition, displaying 267 Congolese people; many became ill and died, and the fate of others is unknown. At Montgomery, we would change over to the 44 tram, would weave through the streets and out of the city, into the Forêt de Soignes – a magical forest of beech and oak trees stretching like long tapered fingers to the sky. Each time the tram reached the forest and penetrated its silky quiet, a spell was cast. We were crossing a threshold, entering a strange new world.

That strange new world was a monument to, and an unintentionally horrifying record of, the colonialist mindset. Meant to provide a window onto the Congo, and an insight into 'the African', it instead unwittingly held up a light to the systematic condescension, acquisitiveness and violence of nineteenth-century imperialism. The tram would emerge from the forest and set us down opposite the museum, where a car park positioned itself around a sculpture of an elephant, the emblem of the Africa Belgium colonised so viciously, its trunk raised triumphantly. The elephant is also the iconic image of Belgium's Côte d'Or chocolate, made from cocoa beans in what is now Ghana, then a British colony called the Gold Coast, by a company founded in the 1880s. In Stromae's video for 'Humain à l'eau' (Person Overboard) – a terse, unforgiving poem of a song about environmentalism, globalisation and race – Stromae dances in a supermarket aisle accompanied by lurid hologram versions of himself; an elephant trumpets periodically.

The main hall of the Congo museum, housed in an imposing neoclassical structure overlooking a glorious lake and parkland, was graced by a more defeated and mournful, though huge, taxidermied elephant. We spent hours, as kids, lolloping around that creature, marvelling at its huge ears, its dejected trunk, its terrifying testicles. I can still smell the museum: an odour of institutions, of polished floors, of musty display cases and of decay. I knew the rooms by heart; the cases to linger over, the ones to avoid. The stuffed animals were fascinating; the pinned insects horrifying. I skipped past the moths, the spiders, the creatures I almost didn't dare examine. There were mocked-up humans holding spears. There were countless photos of 'natives'. There were tired dioramas. There was a great deal to feel uncomfortable about. I remember my mother saying: 'It's stuck in time; it's a museum of a museum.'

Visiting it was to observe colonialism set in stone, embalmed, slowly gathering dust. Yet there was not much at stake for us, for a white family visiting on a day from the city, living a life among the bricks and mortar that were the riches of atrocity. It was not I who was being humiliated by the museum's images, its objects, its very rationale. Eventually, some recognition of this – of the fossilised museum's fundamental partiality – filtered through, and in 2013 it closed for several years, undergoing a substantial reorganisation in the knowledge, finally, that it could no longer fail to critique the colonialism that was once its *raison d'être*.

In the sparse music of 'Humain à l'eau', Stromae speaks in a sort of pidgin French – the kind that French speakers sometimes use when imitating Africans: unconjugated verbs, the language stripped down to its bare, unelaborated components. *You no understand; me explain* – that sort of thing. This naive Afro-French speak is a familiar feature from European caricatures of Africa, not least in the famous Tintin books of cartoonist Hergé – a staple of Belgian childhoods. Also peppered into the iconography of Stromae's act (which is a highly polished, thought-through aesthetic) are the two gormless, neurotic detectives of the Tintin series, Dupont et Dupond ('Thomson and Thompson). The two musicians behind Stromae in his live performances wear bowler hats and an identical get-up – half smart, half boyish – that cannot fail to trigger associations with the lovable fools in the comic books. Stromae plays with a sense of himself as a cartoon character, a cardboard cut-out standing in for the immobile, absent father in 'Papaoutai'. His own Rwandan father was killed in the Tutsi genocide in 1994.

On *Vivement dimanche*, the host Drucker, moved by Stromae's performance, says to him: 'I've been doing this job for fifty years – and I've never experienced that, I've never experienced a moment like that.' He doesn't elaborate; what is it that he's never experienced? Stromae has enjoyed huge praise in Belgium and beyond, and has also endured some formidable projections, by virtue of his history, his skin and his act. He became an emblem of a Europe that would refuse austerity's sectarian hardening; his first big hit, 'Alors on danse', which came out hard on the heels of the 2008 global recession, was a melancholy celebration of music and dance as a retreat from the grinding cycle of unfulfilling work and crippling debt. In his stage shows, Stromae addresses audiences in Belgium – a country which, for all its associations in the English mind with federalism, is painfully, dysfunctionally split along factional lines of language, religion and politics – in both French and Flemish. That this simple gesture is worth noting reveals how deep the linguistic fissures go. Journalists were keen to claim him as their own, a Belgian 'melting pot' encapsulating 'everything of our era'. He became, for a while, a container for all of Belgium's confusion about race and nation; a symbol of the virtues of multiplicity, connection and mixedness against the rise of far-right nationalism in Europe. Commentators, in their exaltation of him, also at times indulged in a fetishisation of his features, of this 'beautiful hybrid'. And yet he looks like the kind of young man that the Belgian police have routinely harassed, the kind that shopkeepers would casually insult to white customers like me.

One can sense, in the adulation of him, the praise upon praise upon praise, a confused mix of feelings. There is a pride about him – and yet pride is often about the person feeling the pride; commentators are implicitly lauding themselves for embracing their mixed progeny. There is also a sense of relief and wonder that a young man, raised by a single mother, with a murdered father, in a riven country beleaguered by its own racism, could rise above the violence or vindictiveness that all this might have engendered. White admiration for him – for his art, for his nuance in the face of political questions – sits troublingly close to a worrying congratulation of him for having turned out so well; for having surprised the gatekeepers. A white audience which praises him, which is tearful as he performs for it, is moved for good reasons – he really is remarkable – but also for dubious ones. Stromae confounds the audience's low expectations of him, an audience that is moved by his reaching the high standards of a culture imagined as white. Stromae, for his part, has in the last few years taken a step back from performing.

I went back to the museum when it reopened to fanfare and scrutiny in December 2018 – its name now the Royal Museum of Central Africa (known locally as AfricaMuseum). A sleek glass building had been constructed to the side of the main neoclassical edifice, within the imposing grounds. This new structure, shimmering and atmospheric, sat atop elegant, minimalist concrete conference and event spaces, deep in the ground. It was linked to the original building by a tunnel, in which one extended stretch was starkly dominated by a pirogue, the long canoe I remembered from my childhood hours in the museum.

At the press conference, the museum's enduring director, Guido Gryseels, spoke of the museum's need to reckon with the past. Journalists asked difficult questions: how exactly has the museum been decolonised? Why not a change of directorship? Why so late, this reckoning? One answer to this last question was a shift of emphasis, after Congo's independence in 1960, away from the museum as an educational resource, towards the institution as a research hub for scholars. The museum, as a result, fell into neglect. And while temporary exhibitions engaged more fully with critiques of empire and scientific racism, the permanent collections remained untouched. This reopening was the fruit, we were told, of many years of reflection and work in response to changing public discourse about colonialism. Various members of the museum staff emphasised the collaborations undertaken with contemporary artists from the Democratic Republic of Congo, whose work was now taking pride of place in the museum; the education projects; the partnership with, for example, the new national museum in Kinshasa; the space given to the history of the institution itself. There is no conclusive position on colonialism, it was pointed out; a cacophony of voices and perspectives would emerge, and individuals could make up their own minds about the past. On the thorny issue of artefact repatriation, for example – the museum has an enormous collection and is attempting to trace which objects were legally and which illegally acquired – 'we are open to discussion', said the director.

The museum was opening to the public in a matter of days. As we went on our tour of the revamped exhibits, workmen were frantically installing, drilling and tweaking while curators paced the halls with headsets. Many of the new features were high-tech, interactive installations that were not quite up and running – we saw quite a few half-empty rooms half announcing their renewed political consciousness. There were many thoughtful exhibits pointing to the scientific racism of early colonial museum practice; photography and its captions contextualised earlier iterations of the very space we were in. Much, however, was unchanged. In the rooms crammed with the artefacts that had made such an impression on me as a child – the lions, the hippo, the leopard, the zebra – the sense of the static, of preservation, of frozen time – intensified for me by this encounter with my past – was stifling. The stuffed animals were less moth-eaten now, but I recognised every one of them. Maps, birds, headdresses and masks were beautifully lit in glorious new cases; everything looked updated, sharper; it was like having one's eyesight corrected. I drifted away from the tour group, suddenly weary from my early rise in London, noticing for the first time the art deco details of the ceilings, the original nineteenth-century paintings of the Congo River on the walls, as I eavesdropped on the conversations unfolding around me. An elderly white couple spoke glowingly of the new cases. A Belgian-Congolese journalist spoke angrily with a friend and I asked her what she made of the revamped space. 'They've made themselves feel better,' she told me. 'It's not a decolonised museum, it's a renovated one.'

She was right. On our journey underground from the press conference in the new glass building to the original neoclassical one, we had passed through a room containing a long plinth, on which a multitude of statues stood crammed together. It looked higgledy-piggledy, as if this were a holding room and the statues were yet to be arranged, artfully, elsewhere. But this was an exhibit, entitled *Hors Jeu* (Out of Play): a room in which the most problematic and offensive images of colonial racism were themselves put on display, but framed as if set aside in the theatre, the spectacle, the game of the museum. Are they out of play, though? In the museum's earlier incarnation, these statues had been dotted throughout the building, without any commentary. The 'new' museum is attempting to provide that commentary; to point to itself, its own history. But, segregated from the rest of the museum, as the statues were in this room, and hastily partitioned off, the gesture seemed flimsy to me, and also telling, unintentionally articulate. We don't know what to do with our shame; let's assemble it all together, cram it into one self-conscious space, underground, and move on. The statues themselves, of course, remained almost unbearable to behold. *Les Aniota* (the Leopard Man) was there – a sculpture by Paul Wissaert commissioned by the Belgian Ministry of Colonies and acquired by the museum in 1913. It depicts a figure from the Aniota, an allegedly cannibalistic secret society with possible animist roots in West Africa. Members were thought to practise ritual murder dressed as leopards, and in the Congo in the nineteenth and twentieth centuries, often of African chiefs deemed too friendly to colonial forces. A malevolent, scheming leopard man features prominently in Hergé's early and staggeringly racist *Tintin in the Congo* (1931). As Jonny Pitts notes in *Afropean: Notes From Black Europe*, Hergé undoubtedly got his knowledge of the Aniota from the museum, where it figures as a conveniently 'savage' emblem of why the Congo needed 'civilising' by its European masters.

Also on the plinth in *Hors Jeu* were several sculptures of slaves: muscular, bulging, their strength fetishised while also being a source of contempt. How should we, either the beneficiaries of racism or its targets, look at these objects? Should we look at them at all? I don't know. But that room was not a solution; instead of a decolonising gesture, it was a splitting one, a gesture of compartmentalisation and denial.

© PAUL WISSAERT
Les Aniota, 1913
Royal Museum of Central Africa

I was born and grew up in Belgium, my British parents' adopted country. I am Belgian and not-Belgian, and I am British and not-British. I barely knew the country my parents came from. It was exciting to me as a kid – our annual trips to relatives were full of unknown exoticisms: Channel 4 and its surreal, knowing adverts, fruit gums, allotments, ancient train carriages with baffling doors (you had to lean out from the inside to open them), people speaking English everywhere. The train from Dover would creak and clank into London, passing the occasional cricket ground in some village in Kent – it would make me laugh as it was both shockingly unfamiliar and iconically recognisable. I felt England unfold before me, scene by scene, as if from some unplaceable film that had been vaguely playing in my childhood, on a flickering TV to which I wasn't paying much attention. Even now, when I return to England after only a couple of days spent in Germany, or France, or Belgium, and my train pulls in to a station with its WHSmith, its Boots, the plastic glare of white and blue, I experience a sharp sensation of being familiar with something by virtue of its unfamiliarity. I recognise a deeply familiar feeling of experiencing England as foreign.

As a teenager, my sense of England was overwhelmingly filtered through the urban melancholy of Morrissey and the Pet Shop Boys: signals from a post-post-punk world, painfully imprinted by the Thatcher years, the dark 1970s. My sense of England was formed by flares from a land that arrived on my TV and Walkman full of strangeness and nostalgia, full of longing and the uncanny. Morrissey standing on bleak, grainy street corners, loafing desultorily in front of Centre Point, singing of the dole and of despair; the Pet Shop Boys walking with detached purpose through dilapidated Soho, two sinister private detectives observing the moral chaos of an unequal society. A society in decay, a decadent world rife with mundane injustices, spinning into destruction. The power-dressing elites gorging themselves on their own excess; the Vicomte de Valmonts and Marquise de Merteuils of the yuppie 1980s, aristocratic teeth bared in their death throes. And the tender nostalgia for the hedonism of youth, for the hedonism of pre-Aids youth; the friends, some here, some no more.

These signals that reached me from England painted it as a place of excitement and drab horror; a place of disintegration, of violence, disappointment and energy. I've never quite shifted that feeling of England, of London in particular: ugly, *jolie laide*, drab, bleak, strange. I need to go home, I sometimes say. It's ugly, I say. I find it ugly. Yes, an English friend said to me once, after a pause, but I guess it's my ugly. Perhaps that's it: perhaps home is the ugliness you can live with and love.

I came to England in 1995, to university, and more or less stayed. Two years ago, I watched Patrick Keiller's *London* and *Robinson in Space*, feature-length essay-films made in the 1990s. They dwell on topography, architecture, vacant lots, roads; Leicester Square, the BT Tower, IRA bombs. The footage, the images, all appeared so familiar; it was as if I was looking back to the 1980s and 90s, but I had barely seen these things at the time; or I had largely seen them through the TV screen, through hours watching MTV, poised to press 'record' on the videotape the moment the Smiths came on.

Watching the Keiller films felt like walking into one of those videos; stepping in, just like the girl in a-ha's 'Take On Me' video, the girl who climbs into the graphic story she is reading, from which Morten Harket beckons improbably. England's past is always on a reel for me. And yet that past is also surging forward, coming back to the future. To live in London now, for the past ten years, has been to feel time going backwards, going back to the shabby streets of central London, the sharp rise in homelessness, that marker of recession and inequality surging all around. Ken Clarke returning to our TV screens, Eurosceptics and Europhobes foaming at the mouth; the present as a *Spitting Image* sketch of the past.

Every time I come back into England, back into London, I have a flash of feeling: why am I here, in this city I love so little, this city of which I am only fond? There's much talk of homelessness at the moment: political homelessness, cultural homelessness; not feeling at home in one's country, in a political party. But who ever felt at home in the first place? Whose home is valued? And whose burns down? 'Each of us knows,' wrote Günther Anders in 1950, 'that our mother is mortal, but none of us knows that our home is mortal.'

Back in the museum, I thanked the curator who had shown us around and made my way out; back to the tram stop, back through the forest, back through the streets of Saint-Gilles and Ixelles, where Stromae roamed as a teenager, going from club to club in search of his musical identity. At the Gare du Midi, I stocked up on my favourite biscuits and made my way back under the Channel, to carry on looking at this home from that one, at that home from this one – at here from there and at there from here. ■

© XAVI GARCÍA
Shhhh . . . the democracy is sleeping, 2013

OFFICE OF LOST MOMENTS

Antonio Muñoz Molina

TRANSLATED FROM THE SPANISH BY GUILLERMO BLEICHMAR

Listen to the Sounds of Life. I am all ears. I listen with my eyes. I hear what I see on advertisements, newspaper headlines, posters and signs. I move through a city of voices and words. Voices that set the air in motion and pass through my inner ear to reach the brain transformed into electrical pulses. Words that I hear in passing or if someone stands beside me talking on a cell phone, or that I read everywhere, on every surface, every screen, wherever I happen to look. The printed words reach me like spoken sounds, like notes I read on a musical score, sometimes trying to distinguish words that are spoken simultaneously or to infer those I cannot hear because they are whisked away or lost in a louder noise. The shapes and fonts give rise to a ceaseless visual polyphony. I am a tape recorder, switched on and hidden away inside the futuristic phone of a 1960s spy, the iPhone in my pocket. I am the camera that Christopher Isherwood wanted to be in Berlin. I am a gaze that must not be distracted even by the merest blink. The woods have ears, reads the title of a drawing by Bosch. The fields have eyes. Inside a dark, hollow tree glow the yellow eyes of an owl. A pair of large ears dangle from a burly tree as from an elephant, nearly touching the ground. One of Carmen Calvo's sculptures is an old wooden door studded with glass eyes. The doors have eyes. The walls have ears. Electrical outlets can hear what we say, according to Ramón Gómez de la Serna.

Perfection May Be Closer than You Think. I go out as soon as it grows dark. It is the late dusk of the first night of summer. I hear the rustle of the trees and ivy in neighborhood gardens. I hear the voices of people I cannot see, eating outdoors on the other side of fences topped with creeping vine or mock-orange, sheltered from the street by thick cypress hedges. The sky is dark blue at the top and light blue on the horizon where the rooftops and chimneys stand in silhouette as in a technicolor diorama. I want to be aware only of what reaches my eyes and ears at this very moment, nothing else. The street is so still that I can hear my own footsteps. The rumble of traffic is far away. In the soft breeze I can hear the rustle of leaves on a fig tree and the slow, swaying sound of the high crown of a sycamore, like the sound of the sea. I hear the whistling of swallows flitting through the air in acrobatic flight. One of them touches the surface of a garden pond so pristinely as it swoops to catch an insect that it does not cause the slightest ripple. I hear the clicking of bats finding their way through the air by echolocation. Many more vibrations than my crude human ears can detect are rippling simultaneously through the air at this very moment, a thick web of radio signals spreading everywhere, carrying all the cell phone conversations taking place right now across the city. I want to be all eyes and ears, like Argos in the myth, a human body covered in bulbous eyeballs and blinking eyelids, or in the bare, lidless eyes on Carmen Calvo's door. I could be a Marvel superhero: Eye-Man. Or a monster in a 1950s science-fiction film. I could be a random stranger or the Invisible Man, preferably the one in the James Whale movie rather than in the novel by H.G. Wells. It is the film, more than the book, that really attains the height of poetry.

Technology Applied to Life. I read every word that meets my eyes as I walk by. Fire Department Only. Premises Under Video Surveillance. We pay cash for your car. There is a kind of beauty, an effortless fruition in the gradual coming on of night. The word *Libre*, lit in bright green on the windshield of an approaching taxi, floats above the darkened street as if clipped and pasted on a black background on a page in a photo album. A glaring, empty bus rushes from the mouth of a tunnel like a ghostly galleon in the high seas. Its entire side is taken by a large ad for gazpacho. Enjoy the taste of summer now. Words fall into a rhythmic sequence. We buy silver. We buy gold. We buy silver and gold. Donate blood. We buy gold. At every bus stop there is a glowing panel advertising a new film. *Gods of Egypt: The Battle for Eternity Begins. Teenage Mutant Ninja Turtles: Out of the Shadows.* There are invitations, commands and prohibitions that I never noticed when I walked down this street before. Do not place plastic containers outside the trash bin. Closed to pedestrian traffic. Enjoy our cocktails. Celebrate your event with us. Long before you walk past the sidewalk tables outside a bar you are met by a murmuring choir of voices and of tinkling glasses and the sound of silverware and china. I go through the thicket of voices and smells without stopping. Roast meat, animal fat, fried fumes, shrimp shells and cigarette smoke. Try our specialties, lamb cutlets, grilled meats. Try our lobster rice. There is a lavish verbal succulence to the lettering on the signs that is not unlike the splendor of a Dutch still life. Croquettes. T-BONE STEAK. *Gambas al ajillo. Callos a la madrileña.* CHEESES. Eggplant and gazpacho. Grilled sea bass. Tuna fritters. Paella. Entrecôte. On a June night, the sidewalks of Madrid have a languorous seaside calm like a beach filled with families on holiday. As I drift along, I realize that this is the last night I will live in this neighborhood where I have spent so many years. A man and a woman, white-haired but youthful, press their faces together and smile in the window of a store that sells hearing aids. Old people in advertisements smile with a certain optimism. Young people laugh and laugh, opening their mouths wide and showing their gums and tongues. I never noticed that particular sign before, its invitation or command, the white letters on a blue ground, the joy of retirees wearing invisible earbuds: Be all ears. Hear the genuine sounds of life.

Go as Far as You Choose. I close my eyes on purpose so that the sounds can reach me more clearly. I sit down on the subway and close my eyes as if I had fallen asleep. I try to keep them shut all the way from one station to the next. I notice the weight of my eyelids, the faint quivering touch of my lashes. When I open my eyes to look around, the faces are even less familiar than they were before I closed them. There is a book in my satchel but I do not read it. I only read the signs I encounter, each in turn, from the moment I hurry down the stairs and push the swinging door. So many things that I never noticed or that I read without being aware of them. Entrance. Shorn of articles and verbs, the phrases become crude robotic indications. *Estación Cobertura Móvil.* Some subway official believes in bilingualism and in literal translations. Station Coverage Mobile. No smoking anywhere on the subway system. Insert ticket. A Public Announcement from the Metro de Madrid. Don't forget to take your ticket. A group of multi-ethnic, multinational youths, grinning in an advertisement. Join the largest design network in the world. One of them is Asian. He wears glasses and looks at the camera. Another is black, with a pierced nose and his arm around the shoulders of a girl who is clearly Spanish. Turn this summer into something unforgettable. Use it or lose it. Exclusive opportunities for those who act quick. Going down the escalator I close my eyes though not completely. For your own safety hold the handrail until you get off. An emergency intercom addresses me with an almost intimate suggestion: Use me when you need me. The city speaks the language of desire. Instead of instantly looking at my phone while I wait on the platform or searching for something to read, I stay on my feet and squint my eyes for a few moments. 'Use Me' was the title of a song I used to like many years ago. One thousand cameras are watching over your safety. At each step there is a new instruction or command. Break only in case of emergency. Don't be afraid to use me, the song said. Commanding voices join the written injunctions. Next train approaching the station. The lack of an article or even a verb heightens the sense of imminence. This is a public announcement. The ground shakes a little as the train approaches. Do not enter or exit subway cars after the sound signal. I look at people's faces and listen to their voices. I am all ears. I move closer to someone who is talking on the phone. Nearly every person in the subway car is absorbed in a cell-phone screen. A tall, serious girl is reading a Paulo Coelho book. Her choice in books is a discredit to her beauty. 'I'll tell you everything,' someone says, right behind me. He leans his head against the glass and he lowers his voice, so I can no longer hear him over the automated message that begins to announce the next station. 'Alright, perfect, OK, alright. See you soon.'

Parrot Could Be Key Witness in Murder Case. Wearily, a woman turns the pages of a free newspaper. Beyoncé unveils outfits for upcoming tour. The train is moving more slowly and quietly now, and I am better able to hear the male voice talking on the phone behind me. He is so close to me that I have no idea what he looks like, this man who now begins to laugh. 'His mother is eighty-seven and she just went to the dentist to get braces.' The Montaigne book is in my backpack but I do not open it or even look for a seat. I am alert, waiting for whatever new instructions will be addressed to me in an imperious or enticing tone. Each passion will take you somewhere. This seat reserved for people with disabilities. Beneath the noise of the train there is a murmur of voices, almost all of them talking on the phone. 'You have no idea how many years I have lived in England.' The voices of people I cannot see seem especially near. 'Neither you nor your siblings must sign anything until you know for sure.' A TV screen hangs from the ceiling. A young man with a shaved head and a black beard moves his lips and the words appear below. I am gay. Then another man, younger, beardless, wearing eyeliner and also moving his lips. I am trans. The face of the man with the shaved head appears again. They flicker back and forth so quickly that their features are superimposed. I am me. And then a third face. I could be you. Live your difference, a purple screen finally says. Another invitation. Another command. Someone must have measured the minimum time required for the faces not to become indistinguishable. A woman is speaking softly but very close to me in a tone of warning or censure. 'He says he's changed, that he wants to come back. But that'll depend on how he behaves.' I try to inscribe in my memory the phrases I hear, the bits and pieces of conversation. Words flow together, blurring and disappearing as soon as I hear them. Forget-It-Fast, says an ad, though I am not sure for what. Words are drowned by the noise of the train or by announcements on the intercom. 'So he's changed? We'll have to see. I don't believe 20 per cent of what he says.' Emergency hammer. I read everything, even the headlines on the pages of the free newspaper that the woman holds right up to my face.

Police Will Know When You Use Your Cell Phone Even When They Cannot See You. Salamanca man beheaded by his eighteen-year-old son. Emergency exit. The great Arctic adventure. I barely notice the faces, just the voices and the printed words. Ringtones. The sharp trill of a text message. Every person is connected to something or someone who is somewhere else. 'I'm on the subway. Just in case the call drops.' When the train comes to a stop, the doors open in front of an advertisement that reaches up to the curved ceiling. For the best family holidays. First-time ocean dives. A new landscape at every turn. A group of young people are jumping off a cliff joyfully into the sea. Some are about to plunge fearlessly and others are already floating against a deep blue. All the fun of summer within your reach. Click for incredible prices. Some reservations cannot wait. Book now. Find out more. Find out now. Buy it now. Try it now. Different messages seem to come from the same voice, the same source, and to be addressed to the same person: me, you. It's me, but it could be you. You, yes, you, says a lottery ad, as if pointing a finger to single you out in the crowd, a face that can see you and has chosen you from a TV monitor. You can be a millionaire. Master the elements with your fingertips. Find the perfect class for you. The woman who was reading the newspaper left it on the seat when she got off the subway car, a mess of crumpled sheets. Join the leading brand in hybrid technology.

Track Your DNA. Get There Sooner. Let nothing stop you. Don't wait until you're down. In just a few years, printed newspapers have lost all their material dignity. Madrid sets a world record in the hunt for Pokémon. They crumple and they fall apart immediately, squalid and superfluous, especially now, in summer. An entire page can be scanned as quickly as a screen. Enjoy a fabulous gourmet experience by the sea. I close my eyes again to hear more distinctly as I let myself be carried along by the motion of the train. The city makes a thousand simultaneous promises. Choose everything. Enjoy it whenever and wherever you like. It is no longer necessary to choose a particular thing and forego what was not chosen. Save while you spend without regrets. Lose weight by eating. Create your custom trip today. I have an old, irresistible addiction to cheap newsprint and the smell of ink. Cannibal fight between hammerhead and tiger shark videotaped at sea by tuna fishermen. We move heaven and earth to bring you the best.

Take a Bit of Our Taste with You. First, all of a sudden, it was that word, REMEMBER, up on a traffic sign on a street I used to walk down every day, but now detached by a chance shift in my attention, which up until the prior instant had been busy with other things – not the ones around me but the ones within me, a sleepwalker suddenly awakened by that visual knell, RECUERDE, forcing me to open my eyes and ears even though I had seen the sign many times and though it is in fact quite common, a metal triangle with a pair of simple black silhouettes, cautioning drivers to a pedestrian crossing outside a school. Remember *what*, I suddenly think. Who is asking or ordering me to remember; what inaudible, printed voice is forcing me to look at something I have seen all my life but that I now perceive as if for the first time, on this sidewalk, this corner, this crossing, the triangle high up on a metal post with its powerful and simple color combination: red along the edge, white on the inside, black for the silhouettes and for the single word in large block letters, REMEMBER. Two children holding hands and carrying satchels, a pair of antique children without backpacks, a boy and a girl who seem to hurry as if they were starting to break into a run. I look more closely and they are indeed running. The satchels in their hands are nearly flung back behind them. Children out of a fairy tale, brother and sister, abandoned by their parents and lost in the woods, or children fleeing an air strike on their way home from school in Aleppo.

Isn't Discovering New Things What Keeps You Alive? You can tell it is an old-fashioned sign because it employs the polite form of address, *recuerde*, in a city where every other voice addresses you informally. In saying '*recuerde*', it also brings to mind the first word of the first verse of Jorge Manrique's *Coplas* on his father's death: '*Recuerde el alma dormida*', let the sleeping soul recall, which is in fact an appeal to the soul to awaken rather than to remember. My eyes seemed suddenly to open wider, my ears too, all at once, as when they suddenly pop from a change in pressure, '*avive el seso y despierte*'. And I began to notice other things as well, momentarily forgetting the path I was on and the dark seething in my brain: I saw a handwritten sign taped to a lamp post, 'Reliable person available for housework and elder care'; I saw a picture of a tanned blonde in a white swimsuit in the window of a drugstore, 'This summer, lose weight when you eat'; I saw a chalkboard sign outside a bar listing the day's specials, 'squid, lentil stew, octopus salad', with a steaming plate of stew skillfully drawn in several colors. Just then, a young woman went by, talking on the phone, waving her free hand so that a loud jingle of bracelets accompanied the imperious staccato of her steps. A woman transfixed by anger, who had no qualms about speaking loudly. 'Mom, she's your daughter. Are you listening, Mom? What do you care what her husband says. There's no reason for you to pay for your daughter's gym. Are you listening Mom? When have you ever paid for anything for me?'

Where Your Fantasies Come True. Ever since that day, I have been on a secret mission when I walk down the street. I used to do it intermittently, if I thought of it on the way to some other task. Now those other tasks are disappearing. They are just a pretext to go out on the street. I do not choose the quickest routes but those that are likely to be more fruitful. I almost never ride a bicycle and I never take a taxi. I walk, or I ride the subway. All my worries and obsessions are dissolved in ceaseless observation. I am no longer my own thoughts, the things that I imagine or remember: just what meets my eyes and ears, a spy on a secret mission to record it and collect it all. I used to check my phone for messages every few minutes. I used to lower my head and scrunch my shoulders, caught in a toxic bubble of gloom, traversing an endless tunnel of mid-morning anxiety. Anxiety was my shadow, my guardian and my double. It kept up with me no matter how fast I walked. It stood beside me as I went down an escalator, whispering things into my ear. It turned the dizziness I got from the medication into vertigo and nausea. There was a morbid magnetism to the muzzle of the train as it came out of the depths of the tunnel and into the station. There was a voice in my ear, inside my head, far back in the nape of the neck, and in my throbbing temples. Now there is no longer one voice but many, a flood of voices, coming always from the outside and as immediate as the things I see, the people going by, the noise of traffic. '*Niña* two pairs of stockings for three euros, *niña*, look, two pairs, three euros.' Expert tailoring alterations and repairs. So that your business can go at full speed. How can I have gone down this street so many times without noticing the river of spoken and printed words I was traversing, the racket, the crowds, the clothes in the window of a dingy store. Wool slippers and orthopedic shoes and shoes for sick children in the window of a store selling prosthetic supplies. Crab, shrimp, huge lobsters in a restaurant's refrigerated display, Gran Cafetería de los Crustáceos, and rows of silver fish with toothed, gaping jaws and glassy eyes. Try Our Lobster Rice, €12 Per Person. The nauseating smell of fish at ten in the morning blending with the nauseating smell of tobacco. ■

REFUGE

Bruno Fert

Introduction by Nam Le

In a way, it's a relief the people aren't there. A human habitation may or may not be more itself with a human in it, but it definitely feels, to an observer, more . . . *available*. After the first photo in this series, which shows scores of migrants crowding a rescue ship's foredeck, people are nowhere to be seen. Throughout refugee camps in Greece, Germany, France and Italy, there are only transient interior spaces, vacated momentarily – by the transients momentarily stationed in them – so someone can step in and take a snap.

That someone is Bruno Fert. And he knows something about invoking human presence through its absence. His previous series, *Les Absents*, portrays the remains of Arab villages depopulated after the founding of Israel; these are haunting photographs, suffused with the ghosts of fled lives – more than 700,000 lives – driven out and denied return.

This series showcases a more intimate kind of human absence. The spaces left behind invite less archaeological reverence than musings on the material culture of modern displacement: here are the standard materials – polyethylene (tarps), polyester (tents), other miscellaneous plastics; plywood and crate wood and scavenged wood; hessian bags branded with the names of international relief agencies; the usual discarded and donated furniture, matting, bedding, clothing, etc. – that constitute basically any refugee camp anywhere in the world in the last half-century. The aesthetic feels timeless because, more than anything, these camps fulfil a function, and that function is timeless.

But Fert doesn't stop there. He's drawn to spaces that vex and tease that function, or mask it, spaces that feature some straight-out head-turners (what we might regard as 'found furnishings'): a proudly upholstered club chair on tamped sand; a lace-curtained rocking bassinet; shack walls covered in Bradford City AFC-branded cladding. And are those really two stuffed tigers? Is that Kermit the Frog riding a black guitar? Ten-up combat boots painted in the style of Fahrelnissa Zeid?

Nothing if not personal. Looking at these rooms, we're forced to scale back from the abstract and statistical to the human, and not just the human but the *specific* humans who have imposed their personalities on these specific spaces. Who have made choices even while making do. (This soft toy put right here; this fabric with that pattern put there, to that purpose.) Who have made an assertion of control even in the knowledge that here, all such assertions are provisional, are subject – just as they are – to the sufferance of the state.

Most of the rooms in these photos have since been bulldozed or burned down. Most of the fixtures and objects in these rooms have been separated from their owners. For me, this charges these objects, and these rooms, with almost unbearable pathos. Imagine having nothing, having already forfeited all your possessions (people smugglers profit by transporting bodies, not baggage), to come by things, and cherish them and make them yours, only to give them up again and again when you move, or are moved, on. Then to prepare, even pose, the next space with pride (the beds are made, the floors swept, tea and fruit proffered), so as to step behind a prize-winning French photographer, watching as he centres in his frame, for the brief blink of a shutter, your marginal existence.

So I'm glad the people are out of shot. People come with demands. Bodies with their gravity, faces with expressions, asking to be looked at, looked away from, looked past. The faces connected to these spaces (shown in Fert's full series, *Refuges*) are all black and brown, belonging mostly to men, often in hoodies and beanies.

Faces, in other words, we've been conditioned to fear. To distrust and despise. (Think how heavily charities lean on images of women and children.) No matter how well intentioned, your first thought looking at the faces of these men would not be 'survivor' or 'victim', and yet these are pretty much the only things – by virtue of their very presence in Katsikas, or Grande-Synthe, or the 'Jungle' in Calais, or the 'Calais of Italy' in Ventimiglia – we can be sure they are. You'd look at their faces and you'd think what you'd think and then, depending on what *you* are, you'd move to confirm or compensate for your bias. Either way, you'd be dealing in conjecture. You'd be drawing tendentious links between human and habitat, you'd be adjudicating narratives: Where did you come from? Why? Are you who you say you are? What have you done? What will you do?

Your gaze, that is to say, would be political.

You can't remove the politics by removing the people. But maybe you can steer your gaze towards a deeper political point. Here's the point I took from these photos: Fert's interiors don't – can't – tell us whether their absent occupants are from Sudan or Syria, Iraq or Pakistan or Afghanistan. They don't tell us their occupants' ethnicities, nor which variant of which Abrahamic religion, if any, they follow, nor which side of which war or feud they fall on, nor how culpable or innocent their participation may have been. They don't tell us whether the occupants are 'genuine' refugees or 'merely' economic migrants.

What they tell us is that these people are (still) people, with their own idiosyncratic interests and tastes. With their strange, specific dignities. With identities (still) unsubsumed by political labels. By focusing on the particular, Fert frames the negative space for a more general point: there will always be conflict; there will always be displacement. These are realities as impersonal as any natural law. To a refugee in a camp, the mechanisms of post-Westphalian states are no less impersonal. States will do what states do, which is protect and preserve themselves, which means (excepting cases of economic advantage) keeping you out. As the news confirms over and over again, the two consistent poles of state policy towards refugees are deterrence and deportation: what happens in between is nobody's business, is 'processing'. (As I write this, the US administration is arguing in court that it has no obligation to provide soap, or a place to sleep, to detained migrant children.) If you're a refugee in a camp, you're out even when you're in; your human particularities don't matter because the camp exists to fulfil the state's function, not your human need.

Outside, inside. These rooms, especially those in the infamous 'Jungle' of Calais, throb with the mania to keep the outside outside. Outside is rubble and mud, ruts, sumps, sand and ash. Burning garbage. Squalor and sewage. Rats the size of rabbits. Hostile traffickers, hostile locals. Outside is fifteen-foot cyclone fencing and tear gas and policemen in riot gear (and even worse, policemen in mufti). Outside you're exactly what they say you are: another ingrate, fouling your own home, but then what else did you expect from these people?

There's one photo I haven't touched on. The last photo in the series shows an apartment room in the 18th arrondissement of Paris. It is flooded with natural light, its wooden floorboards level and beautifully stained. What look like Haussmann windows are recessed and curtained. There is an inset shelf with casing, filled with books and toys, and a board-and-batten chair rail, above which hang ornaments, framed prints. The room is full of such grace notes. It's a well-built room: one that rain wouldn't breach. One, more importantly, that the state could not breach, not without legitimate cause. It occurs to me that home is an embodiment of freedom, and one universally understood and respected. For all the moment's talk of assimilation, I've yet to hear even the most rabid nationalist wanting to dictate how immigrants should adorn their own homes. Inside all is yours, is sacred.

My gaze keeps returning to the top of the photo, to the ceiling cornices with their floral mouldings and fluted dentils. All that intricacy. As if to say: This is about more than function. As if to say: This room will last. You are safe here. You can make plans here. The decorative, in this photo, coming at the end of this series, has never felt so necessary. But that's not right either. The cornices are not merely decorative. Their beauty is part of their function: they disguise and distract from the sites of joinder – the places where different planes meet, the places where all you'd otherwise notice would be warp, leak, lines out of true. ■

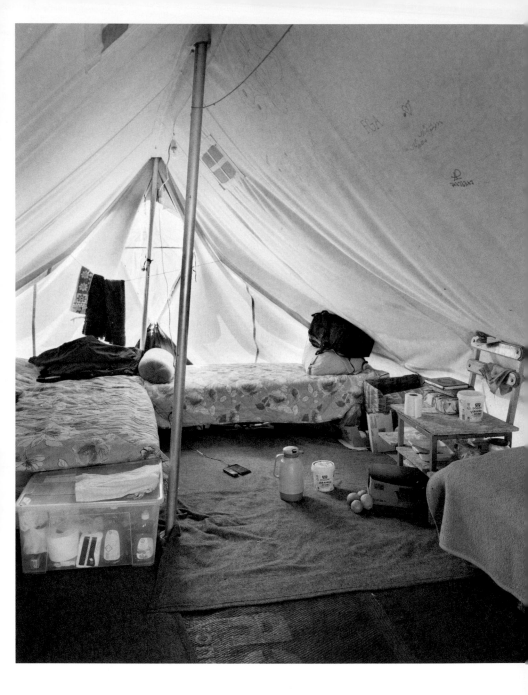

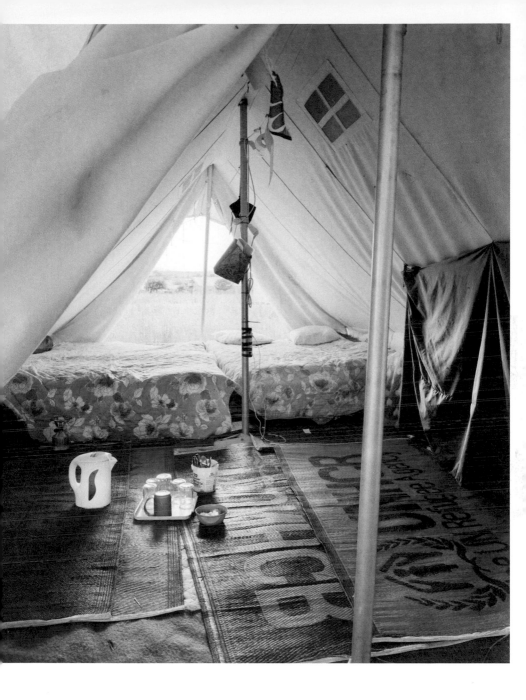

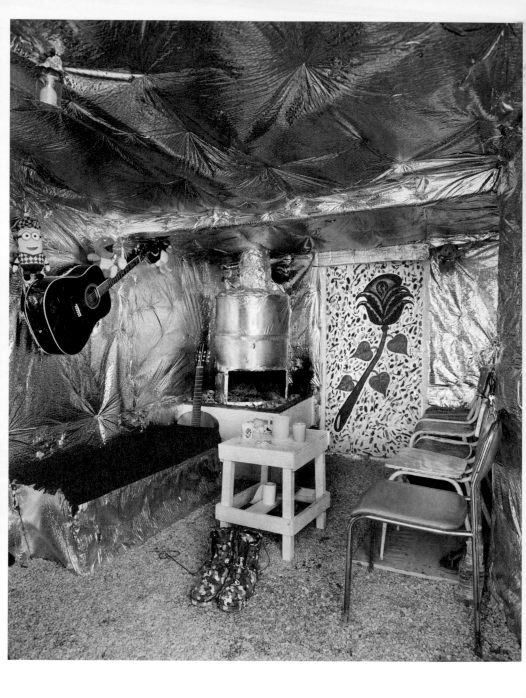

VISITORS REV. 4

Anne Carson

Visitor (*noun*): caller, guest, transient, visitant, habitué (*French*), passenger, newcomer, latecomer, johnny-come-lately (see ARRIVAL).

Friday morning

What are these people doing here? I wake up and the house is full of them. Did I invite them? I don't think so. I listen at my door. How to avoid bumping into visitors on my way to the bathroom. My bathroom is somewhat hidden, maybe they won't find it. Maybe they won't find any bathroom and will go home. I look up 'visitor' in *Roget's Thesaurus*, a handy reference tool I keep in my room.

Reading *Roget's* has its usual calming effect. Words give me – oh I don't know – dangling their little roots in the past as they reach forward, reach towards us. And *Roget's* tidy pages, the beautiful lists, all these analogical children of slight difference – it is the opposite of anarchy! No maybe not. I suppose you know why Roget made lists. Chronic mental instability in several members of his family including himself led him to seek what Freud might have called a *coping mechanism*. Roget made lists of lots of things, not just words. Posterity has not found much use for his tallies of 'things in the garden' or 'the movements of the iris of the eye'. But his *Thesaurus* enjoyed twenty-eight reprintings in his lifetime. He lived to be ninety and dabbled in a variety of scientific researches, e.g. 'Explanation of an optical deception in the appearance of the spokes of a wheel seen through vertical apertures', a paper he presented to the Royal Society of London in 1824, thus more or less inventing the movies.

Freud would have liked Roget.

Friday afternoon

Are you religious? Is this some kind of ritual weekend? I am no longer calm. I glimpsed a woman in white on the stairs. I heard someone rummaging in the kitchen. I descend to confront – a visitor! After the jam? I think so. Or the gin. I don't care about the gin, like to keep the jam for the fox. No! he says, we're making a movie! We'll use seven rooms of the house plus the porch! All at once! Rehearse today, shoot tomorrow! Single take! He is very excited. He talks in exclamation marks like Don Quixote. I ask what the movie's about. Sex divorce fighting longing realness pretending! he says. Not jam? I say and we both laugh. His is a guilty laugh.

Roget had no fox, no fox pocket. Even as a child he couldn't relax, he was compulsively neat. His first word list, compiled at age eight, would continue to be perfected till his death in 1869. He organised the first edition of the *Thesaurus* (1852) in 1,002 concepts. When Roget stared into the fire he was thinking out a problem. Next day by reclassifying 'absence of intellect' as a subcategory of 'intellect' and 'indiscrimination' as a subcategory of 'choice', he pared *Roget's* down to a neat 1,000. Would Freud have liked me? I don't think so. His favoured patients tended to be arty types, girls but not girlish – Hilda Doolittle, for example, who describes her experience of analysis with Freud as the most luscious sort of *vers libre*. Sometimes when they were talking H.D. and Freud let the telephone ring on and on.

We trapped each other, she says, but his wings held. What does that mean? *His wings held.* I'd like to draw Freud with his fox. I'm not good at wings. When not drawing I am incongruous (inappropriate, inapt, improper, incompatible, irreconcilable, inconsistent, unusual, warring, strange, alien).

Saturday morning

My bathroom! As predicted! I stumble in, door not locked, there lies a visitor in the tub in flagrante, guitar on his lap, head flung back to the wall, mouth agape with song, huge naked white foot propped on the taps. This foot projects towards me. This foot is a beachcomber, a beachhead, a beacon, a beast, a bedlam, words fail me. It resembles the dead Christ's foot in Andrea Mantegna's *Lamentation of Christ*, but we know from art history that Mantegna had to scale down the size of Christ's foot lest it block our view of Christ's violently foreshortened legs, torso and face. No scale-down with this guy – splayed out in the bath in his headphones he laughs, he twangs, he flashes his blue eye-guns at me and cries, I love the tension!

Faced with Christ's unforeshortened foot, I retreat to the stairs. What a maelstrom in me. Headphones in the bath! Well, I can't worry about that. Let me just say, these guys are no Éric Rohmer. They claim to be making a movie. Spent yesterday in seven different rooms of the house, not to mention the bathroom, playing and singing louder and louder until by evening the whole place was wailing like a dinosaur. Rohmer wore earplugs while shooting the nightclub scenes of *Full Moon in Paris*, a fine early film of his that (most people don't notice) has a fox in the corner of one scene. 'Éric Rohmer' of course is a pseudonym – his real name being Maurice [something] – his mother never knew he made films, she thought he was a high school teacher all his life. Watch for the fox.

To enter the door of the drawing is uncanny.

93

More on Roget. One morning in 1824 he was gazing out the basement window of his house. Saw a man with horse and cart passing and noticed (vertical blinds) how the spokes of the cart's moving wheels appeared to be curved. He dashed up to the street. Paid the man to drive back and forth several times. Made mathematical calculations. The human retina, he had discovered, typically saw a fast series of still images as a continuous movie. The fox opens and closes in my pocket. Tomorrow the fox will look for the door to enter my drawing.

Did I mention my admiration for Éric Rohmer, I think so. In adolescence I used to watch his movies with pencil and paper in hand, alert for quotes to use with older women. *Oh how he shattered the spirit world, as Pascal said of Archimedes,* is a good one. Also I loved the way Jean-Louis Trintignant pronounced *boy scoot* and his awful haircut. Why am I telling you this? Because Éric Rohmer knew how to make a movie. Keep everybody in the same room, is a good first rule. And who is this woman wandering the halls in white satin undergarments? Do they know her? They demur. Her whiteness makes me dream. She is always going out of rooms just as I come in – it's like living in the New Wave: *I am a bachelor, I am mysterious.*

Saturday afternoon

Sneaking about the halls, eavesdropping here and there, I learn a few things. They are from Iceland, these visitors, which explains a lot. Perhaps you've been to Iceland? I went once, I couldn't stay. There is nothing there but emptiness. A gigantic empty wind wails along the edge of every minute and tosses the odd dazed seabird out onto the empty beach. When you drive the single lonely highway a huge piece of emptiness drives along beside you and goes wherever you go, then piles up in your driveway at home on top of the emptinesses from other days. You see horses standing in the fields so soaked with emptiness they can't move, they've been there for years, they might as well be waterfalls. Of course all this exerts a psychic pressure on inhabitants – the whole soul frays. I made lists while I was there. I took photographs too but later at home found the emptiness had vanished from each one, leaving a tiny print. Pawprint, handprint, mouthprint, I can't tell.

The most uncanny thing about my fox is whether or not he will find the door.

Saturday night

I ask one of the visitors for his theory of mimesis. My heart is a yacht! he cries, quoting some ninth-century saga, no doubt. Then he tells me a long story about his godmother whose name was Engel and who (he claims) knew Freud. In fact Freud invited Engel to his house in London to play the piano. Back in Berlin she had been a popular performer of lieder in sparse modernist arrangements and had been invited by Hitler to do a private concert. *Nein*, said Engel and left for London on the next train. But it turned out Freud had no piano in his London house, only a clavichord. The punchline to this story involves the words 'klavier' and 'komplex' in a bit of Germanic wordplay that he finds so hilarious he loses his balance in the kitchen and knocks over a row of jam jars. There will be a lot of tidying up to do after they leave. Engel made a Freud joke with Freud! he exclaims. The fox is chewing off old bits of the fur behind his leg. His leg is beginning to look like Jean-Louis Trintignant.

But his wings held. I keep returning to this occluded comment. I sense a treacherous nature. And there she goes again, the woman in white satin undergarments, what is she up to? Is she wounded? Is she one of the ten commandments? Is she Engel? Or is she asleep, a dream residue, one of those agile vegetative processes whose activity (Freud says) is doubled as we drift off? Maybe she is an unconscious impulse. Or going back to look for something in the past – the childsoul not yet abrim with sexuality? A better question might be, why is Freud's jargon so catchy? Vernacular, dialect, cant, argot, idiom, lingo, patois,

patter, slang, jive (*slang*), gobbledygook (*colloquial*), technology.
Are children terrifying? I think so – they undress, catch fire, go to
paradise. But they have no power. Freud knew, the fox has the power.

Sunday

My fox gets trembly when there are leave-takings. I'm not sure if he
is sad or glad or just wants jam. The moods of another, this anarchy.
How to reinforce ourselves? Hilda Doolittle's final image of her
analytic time with Freud: him beating his fist on the sofa, saying, I
am an old man, you do not think it worth your while to love me! Eros,
amour, infatuation, crush, flame, passion, desire, attraction, venery,
tender feelings, yearning, devotion, fancy, attachment, adoration,
idolatry, worship, wooing, serenading, romance, intrigue, tryst. So as
the day darkens towards evening I resume my perch on the stairs and
monitor goings-on below. I see all the visitors' souls one by one slide
back into their bodies and scamper off down a grassy slope to the
river. I should return to my drawing but feel a need to check the house
for traces and, so to speak, piss on all the boundaries. Freud in his
heyday would have called this a homosexually-tinged desire. Freud
was prim. In old age he looked like a shrunken monkey, according to
Engel and when she visited him to play his clavichord, he whispered
in her ear, *I was infamous not famous.* Poor rosy-cheeks, what did he
really want? Only the unconscious can track the unconscious. Now
the halls of the house stand empty. Faint ticking or dripping sounds.
Have the microphones been left on? I think so. A tech guy appears,
switching off lights. He goes from room to room. I sit in the dark, I am
patient. Later we will try the drawing again. The fox breathes with the
night, with the stars. In and out he breathes. ∎

'The genius of Europe is what William Blake would have called "the holiness of the minute particular".'
– George Steiner, *The Idea of Europe*, 2004

It was in this way that George Steiner once expressed the essence of the old continent. Europe is a remarkable and rich patchwork of languages and cultures, one smaller than the other. That is easy to see. What is, however, harder to capture is the holiness that resides in our unity in diversity.

Discussing holiness has in recent decades become philosophically unfashionable. The death of God has entailed the death of concepts that originate in religion. Yet the sacred can also have a secular meaning. Rites of passage are still important in the lives of non-believers. And perhaps the concept of holiness too should be preserved and rescued from the dustheap of history.

Holiness is immanent and transcendent: in and beyond the world. Holiness is in a way similar to beauty. An aesthetic experience is not merely a physical, sensory phenomenon. It is also a metaphysical one. Couperin's *Leçons de ténèbres*, the paintings of Botticelli, the poems of Rilke; their beauty is in this world, and opens the doors of perception to a realm beyond.

The minute particular should be revered. We should be wary of the flattening forces of globalisation, when they erase our differences and particularities. Local affinities, sentiments and traditions are not to be dismissed as merely provincial. Neither is the acknowledgement of what binds us decadently cosmopolitan. Europe has proved to be at its best when it embraced unity in diversity. And at its worst when it tried to eradicate that diversity. A telling example is Poland. Some of the most glorious pages of Polish history were written in the sixteenth and seventeenth centuries, when the country did not cultivate the myth of a vast, monolithic culture. Polish territory was a haven of tolerance, where different people with different languages and different religions lived together. We should embrace what is small, for therein lies the grandeur of Europe. ∎

Lara Feigel and her grandmother, Antwerp, 2006
Courtesy of the author

WE DO NOT KNOW EACH OTHER

Lara Feigel

I am alone in my flat where the rain is falling so heavily that I wonder if it will start falling through the fireplace and who I will call on if it does. This is the first home that I've lived in alone, on nights when my children are with their father. The independence is hard-won, but it brings fear: when we do away with the family structure, what do we have to protect us? I am proud of my duck-egg walls, my William Morris window seat, the mantelpiece topped with cherished objects: a Mexican angel, a handmade vase and the menorah looted for me by my father from my dead grandmother's house: an elaborate silver Hanukkah candelabrum that I have never lit. But the elegance and tidiness doesn't hide the precarity of living on my own. Last week, I asked a handyman to install a fire extinguisher in the kitchen and to show me how to turn the household gas off.

In an hour's time, my father will arrive with my seven-year-old son who he's collecting from school, and I'll pick up my one-year-old daughter from nursery. Family life will assert itself, toys will come out of cupboards, this room will be noisy and full of life. In the meantime I sit on my sofa listening to the rain, slouched over my laptop as usual. I tend to write here, or in bed, despite filling a large corner of the sitting room with a stately desk I brought from my marital home. I have moved it six times over the last decade and after its final journey to this flat, the movers said that the back panel would probably break if I tried to move it again. That's fine, I said, we've moved enough now.

It was in the bottom drawer of this desk that I found, a month ago, a red leather diary stacked among the notebooks. It's from 2006, the year of my marriage and the year I met and talked with my paternal grandmother for the first time, encountering that same menorah in her imposing flat in Antwerp. I remember long corridors, cream walls, gold picture frames, dark wood. I was there because my new husband, John, had suggested that we visit his brother Simon in Brussels, and meet my absent grandmother. John had ruptures in his own family: a year earlier his father had seen his own father for the first time in years. John had observed his father's relief after that visit and now took responsibility for connecting me to the grandmother I hadn't seen since she visited us in London just after I was born. Shortly after my birth, my mother gave up converting to Judaism. My grandmother, and the rest of my father's family, cut off contact with us.

When John suggested the Brussels visit, I felt apprehensive. At twenty-six I was still easily embarrassed, and hated the thought of the awkward conversation I would have to have with my father. There were deeper insecurities too: growing up, I had learned to avoid noticing how painful my grandmother's rejection of me felt. I was now fearful of being explicitly spurned. But I'd heard from my father that my grandmother was ill; I knew I didn't have the luxury of years in which to change my mind. So I asked my father for my grandmother's phone number and address, finding that it was in fact possible to talk about her as a living person, rather than the mythological figure he occasionally shuffled off to Belgium to see. His eagerness to help made me think that he'd been hoping I'd ask this for years. For the first time, he told me what he knew about his family's experiences in the Holocaust, a story I'd only heard hinted at. My father told me that he, born in 1941, had been hidden when he was just sixteen months old with a series of three Christian families in Antwerp and Brussels and raised alongside their children. His father and uncle were sent to Auschwitz, and his mother and aunt were sent to Birkenau, where his aunt died.

The facts were so shocking that I found it impossible to imagine. I wanted to ask questions. How had his parents survived? How did they find each other again? And how did they know where their son was now hidden? But I wasn't sure how to ask. We had never acquired the habit of talking about the past, whether because of the trauma of my father's childhood, or the pain of my grandmother's rejection of us, or the newer gaps and silences created by my parents' separation. But though I didn't have the courage to ask questions, my father wanted to talk and he went on to tell me that, after the war, his parents immediately divorced. His mother then married her dead sister's husband and reclaimed her son from where he was hidden, in Brussels. She went on to have two other children: the aunt and uncle I had never met. The family rebuilt their life in Belgium and then, in the 1950s, moved for a few years to New York. They were understandably paranoid and frightened about the implications of the Cold War for the Jews. I was grateful for this conversation. I gathered our wedding photographs and my first book, a literary anthology of smell, and set off to knock on my grandmother's substantial door, offering myself as an unwanted gift.

Diary
3 December 2006, Sunday, 11.30 p.m., Brussels

Sitting in the 'dining room' in Simon's dusty flat in Brussels whilst John and Simon watch the news. Need to concentrate and write about my meeting with Granny Hilda today before I forget anything.

Phoned this morning 10.30 a.m.

'Hallo?'

'Hello, I am Lara. Marcel's daughter.'

'Vat?'

'I am Lara. Marcel's daughter.'

'Vat do you vant?'

'I am on holiday in Belgium and am coming to Antwerp

today and would very much like to come and see you, just for a coffee, if you would like . . .' Drift into silence.

'Here is my son.'

I explain my case to George. They talk Yiddish in the background. I hear him say 'Marcel's *tokhter*'. He seems to say she doesn't have to see me. He comes back to the phone. She will see me, what time? What time does she want? More discussion. 3 p.m.

John and I arrived in Antwerp at 1 p.m. Ate mussels and settled him in the hotel next door to her. I rang the bell punctually at 3 p.m. It rang but I heard nothing. I went into the inside lobby. Rang again and waited. Saw the lift going up and then down. A woman (fortyish) comes out. Friendly. In the lift I ask if she's George's wife. She speaks no English. Must be the maid.

Hilda comes to the door. Elegant. Well dressed. Strange ill-looking pale blue eyes. We hold hands briefly. She is pleased to see me. Formal. Fusses to the servant about the (instant) coffee. It should be stronger. Asks me. I am prepared to drink caffeine and am grateful it is weak. She takes me into the sitting room – elegant, fussy. Changes her mind. There are two of us. We'll drink in the kitchen. She is shaky (health? nerves?). She tells me she is very sick. Paralysed in the leg. Already? No but she can feel it and they have said there's nothing they can do. Nothing? I only half believe her but am sympathetic. She asks (actually slightly earlier) who I am in Brussels with. I say 'My . . .'

'Boyfriend?'

'No, actually, husband.'

'Oh. You are married at last. That is better.'

Later – more amicable – in the sitting room:

'Why you take so long to be married?'

'I wanted to be sure.'

'Oh yes. That is better. Not like your father. He made a mistake.'

'But he . . . wasn't good at being married.'

'Ah yes. He is better alone.'

'And it's better he married when he did. He has something.'

'Yes. He has you.'

Anyway, the kitchen table. It is awkward and she makes it more awkward with her comment 'You see. We do not know each other. We have no conversation.' Sad, not accusing; but what to say?

I bring out photos and my first book. She is reluctant, but then pleased. The book – solid, hardback, and the name – 'Feigel' – there on the front. It doesn't matter what the book is. But it's the photographs that melt her. She doesn't recognise Daddy and then is pleased that he's so smartly dressed. I am proud. She says 'You love your father, yes.'

'Yes.'

'Yes, I can see that.'

She thinks that I am beautiful in the photos. She is drawn to beauty. John is handsome.

'You are happy, yes?'

'Yes.'

'Yes, I can see that.'

I think it's before we leave the kitchen that she starts referring to the past. To my mother, who was beautiful. She is not apologising yet. She asks about John. What does he do. 'Oh yes, architect. That is good. There is always vork.' About Marcel. I say he's busy. 'Ah. That's good. He has vork.'

'Some.'

'He has enough money?'

I move my hands to say so-so.

'You help him?'

'I try.'

You should help him, I want to say, but don't.

Into the sitting room. She shows me photographs. Her children. Her grandchildren. They look like small-town

American Jews. Plump, well fed, satisfied. Then her parents, dead before the war. 'They were very religious. You have to understand. They were very religious. That is why I could not see you.' I ask for photos of Daddy ('Marcel') as a child. She doesn't have them handy. 'You have not seen them. He does not have them?' No. Another time.

We sit down. It's still awkward, and she mentions it again. She says George is coming. Should she hurry him up? He's always late. So's Marcel. We share a Marcel-is-always-late moment. She calls George: 'You have to hurry. She's about to leave.' Then somehow knowing that time is limited it gets better. She talks about my mother and how beautiful she was. 'But I saw a photo of her a few years ago. She has changed.' It's as though her beauty almost justified her lack of Jewishness, but not quite. Hilda's version of the story is that Mum started converting and then got ill and stopped. I agree. She asks if I have any Jewishness. I say, lying, that I went to synagogue a bit as a child but then wasn't taken any more. NB all this in pigeon English, so much more difficult than it sounds. And her: 'Your English is perfect. Too perfect for me. I cannot understand you.'

The maid is there. She likes the photos. Says I am beautiful. Hilda is proud. She spends a lot of the time staring at me, and saying at intervals how like Marcel I look. I agree. She says I must understand her. She had a difficult life. And Marcel. He had a difficult life. Does he talk about it? No. 'He will as he gets older.'

She starts talking. About how he was hidden. What it's like for a mother to leave her first newborn son. How whenever the trains arrived at the concentration camp she would look anxiously for Marcel. Then at last when he was five years old she went to fetch him and he didn't want to come with her. Her love for him, as she said this, was utterly unmistakable and convincing. I think the main good thing to come out of the visit was to realise that he had been loved. Then she started to talk about her own time in the camp. She was alone. Her sister was sent straight away to the gas chamber because she had asthma.

Then George arrived and everything changed.

He was shown the book. Impressive but the paper was brown. 'Why is it brown? It looks like an old book?' Then he realised it was an anthology. I didn't really write it. Then the wedding. Why Greece? Who married us? I mention the registry office in London and then the blessing in Greece. Who by?

Me: 'A Greek . . .'

Him: 'A Greek . . . Orthodox priest?'

Me: 'No, no. A Greek . . . Mayor!' Triumphant. Just convincing.

He asks about London. A pompous man of the world, comes to London every few months. Is not embarrassed to admit doing this and not seeing us. Mentions a property he could have bought in Canary Wharf. Only 36K. And Granny Hilda, oblivious, staring, saying I look like Marcel.

George is struck by John's height in the photos. Asks it in metres. I say two metres. He is impressed. Asks where he is. I say the hotel next door. It takes Hilda a while to understand this but she is pleased he is waiting: 'He is a good husband.' She doesn't want him to come up though. She is too sick. The whole conversation is punctuated by how sick she is. 'I thought I was about to become happy but instead this happened. I am sick.' George ignores her. Then at the end she says again, 'They say I will be paralysed' and George starts interrogating her. 'Who is they? You haven't told me this.' 'I . . . I didn't tell you?' (Hesitant.) 'No.' He is breaking her. It seems unnecessary. Let her have her pity. She deserves it now. But he is given a different complaint every day. He cannot pity her.

He fusses about a tray the maid put coffee on. It is too valuable to use. It is part of his collection. He puts it on the mantelpiece proudly, pompously. She is oblivious, frail.

It is time to go. His wife is coming and we will collect

John from the hotel to see Antwerp. She tries to feed me. A sandwich? She's anxious about the lack of food. An apple? I accept the apple and she fetches it with a plate and knife, which I use. I am good at cutting apples and hope to impress her.

She asks if I have seen and liked Belgium. The weather has not been good; I am unlucky, like her earlier (I told her she was lucky to escape the concentration camp – she said, 'I was lucky. But now I am unlucky'). I mention her holiday house in Knokke. She likes it. I like cycling. They cycle there. I suggest I come. She likes the idea. George is enthusiastic. She thinks she may be too sick to go this summer. A plan is half formed, though.

We stand up to go. She takes my hand and says she is pleased I came. I say I am pleased. She is obviously regretful. I am emotional. She says 'I love you' out of the blue; direct, childlike. I burst into tears. George lingers discreetly in the sitting room with the maid. She starts hugging and kissing me. On the cheek, the neck. She is more affectionate than I could ever have imagined her. Calls me 'pookie', says 'You are *sensible* [French pronunciation] like your father.' She seems to overflow with love. She says she is sorry for what she did. I have to understand. She did it for the family. How could George and Marilyn's children hold their heads high if they had a non-Jewish cousin? But times are different now. There is more intermarriage. She regrets what she has done.

'How old are you?'

'Twenty-six.'

'I have wasted twenty-six years when I could have known you. I didn't know what you were like.' George comes in. She says to him 'You see what I have given up. I haven't known her. And it was for you. For the family.' She says, as though to make up for it, that normally no one is allowed to come and see her. That she let me come. Then, more emotional, that now her door is always open to me. I promise I will come back.

I remember I have a camera. George offers to take a picture

of us. She clasps me to her, clinging, as though she doesn't want to let me go. I am crying as I write this, silently. John is laughing at the television in the other part of the room, his brother now in bed.

Then I left. Collected John, anxiously whispered to him that we were married by a mayor, and took him to meet George who was collecting his wife. The walk with them was anticlimactic, odd. George was a Jewish stereotype in a different way from Hilda. Obsessed by money. Impressed John was an architect. George told John about the flat in Canary Wharf ('It kills me'). They walked us to the bridge and back and then for coffee in the station. Anxious to show John the building work in the station. Then at the end 'Regards to Marcel.' I can see how he puts Daddy down every time he comes. I want to be at a family dinner with John so that we can defend Marcel. Can show that he's worth ten of George. Which I think in a way Hilda realises, I think she misses him, is sad about whatever happened between them. It's sad – it seems like it wouldn't be too late for any of us if it weren't for her Alzheimer's, but as it is it's almost pointless – to forge a new relationship that she will only forget.

I wanted to write about *Perfume* which we saw this evening. Showed that literature is better than film to portray smell. Will write about it tomorrow.

This diary entry is comprised of nine pages from a reporter's notepad, stapled into the red leather diary that I hadn't taken with me to Belgium. The handwriting is neatly looped, modelled in adolescence on the writing of a girl I admired at school. She was, as it happens, Jewish, as were more than half of the girls at my school: Jewish girls who didn't think of me as Jewish. It makes me cry when I read it, as do many of the entries surrounding it, recording the minutiae of the marriage that I committed to with such determined optimism. I am, as Hilda said, *sensible*, sensitive despite my briskness. And so, it seems, was she.

Reading the diary, I must come to terms with the feeling of helpless anger that surfaces in the writing alongside the sadness that I found easier to acknowledge at the time. My 'pompous' uncle, those cousins I dismissed as 'small-town American Jews': I seem to have felt that within the competitive family dynamic, I needed to lash out at the Belgian relatives in order to defend my father. There had been years of exclusion and I responded in the only way I knew, attempting irony and literary laceration, because in the act of writing I could overcome my helplessness and be in control. It makes painful reading because the anger feels so hesitant. I suspect that I would have stopped dismissing them if only they had accepted me, as I had longed for them to do. My yearning is there in that peculiar epithet 'Granny Hilda'. I suppose it was my parents who'd decided in my childhood that my grandmother should be known by that name, but in retrospect it was a very odd way to describe this French- and Yiddish-speaking woman. I must have known that as I wrote the diary, yet I persisted in using that misleadingly cosy and English appellation because what else could I call her? I clung to 'Daddy', to 'Granny Hilda', a child in need of protection despite the almost-convincing nonchalance of my writerly voice.

The diary has brought Hilda's flat into my flat, and inside it there's the ghost of the flats that my father was hidden in for the first five years of his life. The flats squeeze in like Russian dolls. And there are other flats crowding in here too, because in bed at night, under the neat cream quilt with which I attempt to bring order into my world, I have been watching the Israeli TV programme *Shtisel*, a surprise hit about Orthodox Jews in Jerusalem, living in an inward-looking community that feels like a contemporary ghetto. On the small screen I hold in my hands, people who could be my relatives join me in all their madness and splendour, and I in turn wander among them, a tourist in the world of my family. Immersed in the Orthodox tradition of covered flesh and softened colours, I've been struck by the shock of a naked arm or a brightly hued dress when the characters drive into town. It's made me aware of how bright I must have looked to

Hilda that day, arriving in my light-blue coat and scarlet scarf. And how exposed I must have looked among the women gathered in the garden at my cousin's flat in north London, which I visited shortly after Hilda died.

This was George's daughter Nathalie, who turned out to live only a couple of miles away from us in Finchley. We were there for a hair-cutting ceremony – the *upsherin* performed on three-year-old boys. It was a hot day but the sitting room was crowded with suited men, pressing in on a small child with a pair of glinting scissors, each cutting a lock at a time, reciting prayers. I thought it was barbaric: it reminded me uncomfortably of circumcision. I retreated to the garden with my baby, joining the other women and children. I felt safer among my sex, but turned my awkwardness into haughtiness, pitying Nathalie for her wig-wearing life among these uniformed friends and relatives. My father and John loitered in the corridor, unsure which group to infiltrate, as relieved as I was when it felt possible to depart. Why wasn't I more curious, I wonder now, more admiring of Nathalie's courage in allowing her friends and religious leaders to encounter this peculiar, clumsily ignorant contingent of her family for the sake of strengthening the blood ties?

And what did I expect, that day in Belgium? It's hard to recapture now, but I think I hoped that they might just forget why they had cut me off. Perhaps they would have done, perhaps her door really would have remained open, that stately flat suddenly exposed to the world, if she hadn't deteriorated so rapidly afterwards. I thought that it was their responsibility to become more tolerant and more open to my world; I don't think I was that interested in finding out about theirs. And yet. In the years that followed, sitting in a well-upholstered library in Mayfair, I wrote two books about the Second World War. I witnessed the suffering of Billy Wilder, who compulsively watched hours of footage from Bergen-Belsen, looking for signs of his own lost mother and grandmother. I witnessed the liberation of Dachau through the eyes of a devastated Martha Gellhorn – she couldn't believe what she was seeing: ageless, faceless skeletons in the sun, searching for lice. Surely I was picturing my grandmother among those ravaged women. But I only allowed the Holocaust to slip in at the edges of my writing.

Recently, some friends told me that their marriage was based on a shared sense of the Holocaust; the fact that most of the people in both their families had been murdered. It was a provisional thought. She said it first, trying it out, using me – as they often do – as audience or adjudicator. He agreed, tentatively, that it had been the extermination of their ancestors that had brought them together. This made no sense to me. I escaped back to a world where relationships are built on the future you'll have together rather than on the past you didn't share. But since reading that diary entry I'm wondering about all these questions. I am so grateful to my then husband for suggesting we go to Belgium in the first place, for waiting patiently downstairs in the 1970s interior of that hotel, for performing for my new uncle the two metres of worldliness that I needed from him. Perhaps, though, our marriage would have been stronger if our worlds had not been so far apart. I think of the years that followed: increasingly, we were unable to see the best in each other, unable to take on each other's faults and weaknesses as parts of the person we loved. I wonder what experiences his family would have had to endure for him to cry with me that night in Brussels instead of laughing at the television.

It's a thought I dislike, even as it occurs to me: there must come a point when we can stop looking back. During all the recent debates about Europe, it has bothered me that the case we make is so dependent on the bombed cities and living skeletons of 1945. Yet now, in this defiantly forward-looking flat, my past confronts me. It's there in the diary and in the menorah, but also in the figure of my son, who is about to ring the front doorbell. Witnessing the abrupt highs and lows of his days makes me surprised that I remember as little as I do from my own life as a child. I've started to wonder if this blank relates to the blank where the collective memories should be: life flattened out.

Talking to my son also makes me realise how much I must have cared about my wider family at his age, and the effort that must have been required to stop caring. My son counts his grandparents, his great-aunts, his cousins, ranking them in order of favourites. He takes pleasure in this roll call of people whose existence somehow makes his existence more inevitable. This feels distantly familiar, and I wonder how I handled those conversations with my childhood friends. At some point, probably as an undergraduate, I started dismissing the whole notion of blood ties as a false ideology. How much better, I said, to commit seriously to friendships with people you've chosen rather than devoting your energy to relatives who are foisted upon you. Certainly, I committed to friendships with the kind of passion many people save for relatives and partners. But isn't it telling how much I needed those friendships to resemble family ties? I have honorary sisters, honorary mothers, honorary grandmothers. Even the dead writers I've most admired have been co-opted as unwilling ancestors.

I am going out later so I choose a dress from my wardrobe, thinking of my grandmother's love of beauty, and how unexpected I found it at the time. I can see now why you might desperately hold on to beauty when you've seen it destroyed; why you might care about the easy signifiers – health, height – willing them to be portents of strength. And I suppose it's a characteristic I share, however much I mocked it in the diary. Is that what family is for? Helping you to understand what formed you? 'You are *sensible*, like your father.' Those rooms – the kitchen where I ate the apple, the sitting room where we examined the photographs of her dead relatives – were rooms my father paced, talking awkwardly, angrily, sadly, for decades. That city, where we observed the architecture as tourists, was the city where a mother had taken her baby son to another woman's house, knowing she would probably never see him again; where she had collected him four years later only to find that he had acquired a new mother. She had to wrench him from her as abruptly as she'd been forced to abandon him in 1941. After the war, a new family came jerkily into being, stumbling against the ghosts of the recent dead.

Rushing home each night to watch another episode of *Shtisel*,

I've been using those invented characters to understand myself. I've realised that my father's love of routine, which I've inherited, is a way of establishing ritual. To return to particular cafes on particular days of the week, to swim at particular times in particular places – if you're used to going to synagogue every morning, to reciting certain prayers at certain times of the day or year, then how much must you need these alternative rituals to ground you? I think of the Sunday afternoons and evenings I passed as a child in the sitting room of his small, sparse flat, presided over by a desk even more magisterial than mine. Each week we watched *The Cosby Show*, taking refuge in the fantasy of a large family, energetic and benign, and then ate the same selection of raw vegetables for dinner. This was our sabbath, our week nearly as sacral as the Jewish week. In the past, I've thought of our insistent habits as a form of control, warding off the uncertainty and chaos we might otherwise be faced with. But perhaps there's something closer to life's essence in this. At one point in *Shtisel* the patriarch tells his son not to make so much fuss about his choice of bride: the important thing is to marry, and then to get on with life. It's a new thought for me, but an enticing one: that life may be located in our routines and rituals, rather than in the mind that experiences and analyses them.

I think of my father when he was my son's age, singing the prayers in synagogue while his mother sang them in the women's section upstairs. This was all they had, after the war, the faith in the sovereign ruler of the universe who had made them free. What else could they do but obey those laws; what else could she do but continue to obey them, even when it cost her the loss of a granddaughter in whose particular combination of impatience and sentiment she would later recognise a kindred spirit. I don't know if she succumbed in the end to the paralysis waiting outside the opened door; I have never asked my father if she lost all feeling in that leg. Perhaps she didn't. Perhaps the opened door was enough to prevent it. Perhaps a door half open is all any of us have to hope for, or to offer. ■

'But worse than all else about Europeans is their slovenliness! The Kirgiz in his yurt has cleaner habits (even cleaner than those in Geneva). I am horrified. Before, if someone had told me this about Europeans, I would have laughed in his face. But the devil take them! I detest them beyond all measure!'
– Fyodor Dostoevsky in a letter to A.N. Maikov, 1868

Dostoevsky loved Russia and hated Europe, where he spent about four years of his life. It was in Europe that he restored the state of his health, gambled away his money in a German casino, and all the while yearned for his homeland.

Slovenliness is the least of his reproaches against Europeans. Other sources of dissatisfaction were far more profound:

> Their mores are altogether primitive. If you only knew what they hold to be good and what they consider evil. Meanness, backwardness: the drunkenness, thievery, and petty fraud that govern their trade practices . . . (In Germany I was most astounded by the stupidity of the people; they are unspeakably stupid, immeasurably so) . . .

About five years ago, I published an article in Austria entitled 'Goodbye, Europe!'. The premise of the piece is that, starting from the time of Peter the Great (who reigned from 1682 to 1725, and accomplished tremendous reforms), Russia has vacillated between an urge towards greater social and cultural proximity to Europe, and alienation from it. It seems clear to me that during the past ten years, Russia has reached the apex of its estrangement from Europe.

The views I expressed in my article caused a storm of indignation, which, I must admit, surprised me. It turns out that a large number of my compatriots are of the opinion that Russia is travelling a 'third' path – neither European nor Asian, but rather an idiosyncratic one, a path peculiar to Russia. In a certain sense, this notion is justified: seventy years of Soviet and post-Soviet power did, indeed, represent a third path. A Soviet one.

From our vantage point in the present, it is difficult to know whether Dostoevsky would have accepted the Soviet system; and, more poignantly, whether the Soviet system would have accepted him. He died in 1881, nearly four decades before the new dispensation was established and some of his novels banned.

Dostoevsky was a great Russian patriot. He did not like Europe. And he has many kindred spirits in Russia to this day. Last year, during a talk, I said in a rather offhand way that Russia was lagging behind Europe by about 150 years. I actually think that in some respects it lags behind by well more than 150 years. But how much vehement backlash there was! The most striking response was from a gentleman who insisted that Europe had received from Russia not only its knowledge of hygiene, but the sewage system itself.

It's hard to know how to answer a person who is both ignorant and speaks with unassailable self-assurance. Would he believe me if I told him that the first sewage system was discovered in the city of Mohenjo-daro, and dates from around 2500 BC? Or that in ancient Rome, the sanitation system known as the Cloaca Maxima was laid six centuries before the birth of Christ? The first sanitation system in Moscow went into operation in 1898. According to official data, 26 per cent of households are still not connected to a central sewage system in present-day Russia. People answer the call of nature, summer and winter, in a wooden outhouse that stands some distance from the main dwelling. Any trip to the outhouse is especially daunting during the long winters.

How can these circumstances be reconciled with Dostoevsky's attitude towards the shocking slovenliness of Europeans? How can they be reconciled with his decision to undergo treatment for illness in Europe?

All in all, this is one of the secrets of the celebrated 'Russian soul': the aversion to Europe.

Dostoevsky was an inspiration for this kind of aversion, which is still common among the more ignorant and uneducated Russian patriots. And the more highly educated, prosperous patriots? No problem – they buy houses in Europe, and are never heard to bemoan European standards of hygiene. And they don't need to travel to Kirghizia to take advantage of its cleanliness. ∎

Translated from the Russian by Polly Gannon

GRIEF'S GARDEN

Caroline Albertine Minor

TRANSLATED FROM THE DANISH BY CAROLINE WAIGHT

O n a bench in Enghave Park, we just gave up. As I sat and watched him limp off in his black half-length coat, I felt a deep urge to shoot him in the back. I wanted to see him collapse and lie unmoving in the gravel. A parody of a human being, though I was the inhuman one. I could barely make myself treat him with respect – just hit and bit and spat and kicked. In the year since the accident, I'd destroyed an antique magnifying glass, our door, a book of Milo Manara's drawings and several of his sweaters. Returning to the shop we'd left empty-handed, I bought a harmonica and a jigsaw puzzle for our son.

We were spending Christmas together, for all our sakes. He gave me two bottles of red wine and *The Hosier and Other Stories* by Steen Steensen Blicher. Me, five years ago: aged twenty, doped up on love and sex, my head on his chest as he reads me 'The Gypsy Woman' in our bedroom, which looks out onto the overgrown garden. His voice isn't cracked yet. It's composed, and rather lighter than you'd think to look at him – he's tall and dark and broad, my M, with a thick beard and a vaulting forehead. He read me 'The Gypsy Woman' one evening when we first got together. But he doesn't remember that now. The memory exists in me alone, and he must have bought the book because he knows *he* likes Blicher. He asked me to open my presents before dinner, as though eager to see my reaction. Or maybe he wanted to spare his family? Maybe he was thinking that far ahead. I sat at the kitchen table and tore the paper off the first, then the second bottle, leaving the book till last in the hope that it would rescind the insult of the wine. It was disappointment that tightened my throat as I thanked him. My father-in-law put his arm around me and led me upstairs, into his office. There, love, he said, and I cried into his soft shoulder. There, there.

I go down to the water and follow it. Quarter past seven on 24 December – there's nobody else on the street. Out above the sea it's blue and spitting. At the fort I see a family with five children, speaking a language I don't understand. As they climb the steps towards me, I sit on a bench and rock to and fro to the sound of my own breath. They don't slip on the wet steps, their faces bright against the darkness and their black hair. Did she give birth to all five? I'll never be able to kill myself, I realise. This is the closest I'll come, but I'm still a long way off. By the time I get back to the others, the roast duck is on the table and nobody asks where I've been. M is pleased with the gloves and the extravagant whisky.

The neuropsychologist at Department 123 concluded one of our brief and useless meetings by quoting a Chinese proverb. *You leave grief's garden holding a gift*, he said, but he didn't answer when I asked what happens if you prefer to stay.

That day in Enghave Park marked five years, six months and fifteen days since I took a job as a receptionist at the architecture firm, since the first time I saw and fell in love with M, nine years older, across a high-ceilinged model-making workshop; two years and seven days since I gave birth to our son; and one year and four days since his father hit his head – first against the taxi's windscreen, where it left a cobweb break in the glass, then against the asphalt, with such force that his brain ricocheted inside his skull. The worst part isn't the blow, they told me later. It's the recoil. I had a missed call from the man who found him. The sheer thought. The screen on my phone lighting up in my bedroom, him lying on the wet roadway as I continued to sleep. The sheer thought.

The officers used my name a lot. Maybe that is something you learn at police training college. My name like a hand reaching into the dread and holding me upright by the collar: *Put your clothes on, Caroline, and come downstairs, Caroline, we'll drive you to the hospital. Put your clothes on and come downstairs.* I was too shivery for socks. The feeling of my bare feet in trainers in December, my breasts, soft from nursing, sticking to my stomach beneath the woollen jumper. The two men were ordinary, clean, dressed alike in dark blue turtlenecks with gold buttons at the shoulder. One of them asked if I was going to vomit. The other sat in the back seat and took my hand. I'd been to the hairdresser's that day, and when M and I had sex afterwards I'd briefly felt as though there were some third person, heavily perfumed, with us in the bed. In the waiting room at the trauma centre I could smell the products in my hair again, feeling the prayer rise inside me like steam and sickness. To fill the time with something other than horror, I recited it ceaselessly. *Don't let him die | I'm not finished learning | I'm not finished loving,* I prayed, *Don't let it be him | Let it be someone else.* Could I transmute that body? Swap it at the last second for some random stranger's? He lay naked under a sheet on the hospital bed. That was his urine in the matt plastic bag, the smell of the party still on him. Kissing his forehead and cheekbone, which glittered with asphalt but hadn't yet swollen as it would do overnight, I scolded him softly. You promised me this. You promised me that.

The next few days, as I sat and watched M among the machines, I was afraid of more than simply losing him. Over the years I had fused myself with him, as surely and unobtrusively as a Siamese twin, and in his motionless body I saw my own decline. I didn't doubt the vital organs were his. I was the parasitic twin, the growth. If he left me, it wouldn't be long before I dried up like a child's umbilical stump.

As soon as the consultant removed the drip which kept him asleep, a quivering began beneath his eyelids, his legs stretched spastically and his mouth tasted itself. He coughed, frightened, his muscles trembling and twitching. I imagined his journey out of the coma as an increasingly painful ascent through dark water. Putting my face close to his, I whispered without conviction that he shouldn't be afraid.

His hands fumbled for the tube in his nose supplying his brain with extra oxygen, and the nurse had to bandage them. The hands I knew so well (even now I can see them before me, doing anything, and everything), compressed into two bound lumps. It upset me to see them waving in the air in front of his face, like cat's paws or tiny boxing gloves.

The officers came to the ward and dropped off a plastic bag with the cut-up woollen coat. Inside, apart from his phone, I found an orange dummy, the nutmeg (an amulet) and a note I'd long ago secreted in the smallest of the inner pockets. The paper had rubbed thin and soft along the cross fold, and I envied the hands that had made those creases at a bar in Amsterdam four years earlier.

Someone had written his name and *welcome* on a board outside room 93. He slept a lot in those first weeks, and his waking gaze was blurred by sedatives. The therapists had built him an oversized playpen, a fence of blue mattresses held in place by two low cabinets. I lay down next to him and burrowed under his arm, trying to distinguish his sweat-scent from all the rest of it. Chemicals leached through his pores, his skin flaked with eczema and his breath smelled metallic. He was a thousand worlds away, caught in vivid, swirling hallucinations. He was in Berlin. He was in Santiago. He was a guide at the science museum, nineteen years old again, then twenty-eight. There were animals everywhere. He caught fresh fish and ate them on the shores of a lake, offering me a piece of cod, and the birds had broken their wings. They had to be taken to the animal hospital. I was a dirty whore, I was his Japanese intern Natsuko. Recognition would shoot without warning across his face like leaking current, before it was gone again and I could be anybody.

For years his old apartment had been rented to a Czech family. Every so often they invited us to dinner. I remember dishes like chicken in orange sauce, yogurt with red berries and strudel filled in the middle with a sweet poppyseed paste. When Kristina became pregnant with their second child, they found somewhere bigger and

M put the apartment up for sale. The contract had been signed a few days before the accident. The young woman who lives there now has a limp handshake and a silver lamp in the window where M's wiry basil plant used to stand. Her father kept messaging me while M was in hospital. I'd told him that the previous owner of the apartment was in a coma, yet day after day he continued to send me lengthy messages about keys to the attic and a gate I didn't know existed. *We've got to sort this out*, he wrote, and I decided to let them see me. There were the same stairs where I'd slipped and fallen a few years earlier. Nothing had actually happened, but M had come home from work, and to be on the safe side I lay down on his bed. The problem was that I couldn't stop laughing. I laughed so hysterically and continuously that he phoned the emergency doctor, who asked to speak to me, and after that I fell silent and went to sleep. It was only shock. The whole family answered the door: the limp, blonde-haired girl and her parents, their faces flecked with paint. I gave the father a handful of keys I'd found at home – I can't throw keys away, keeping them all without exception in a sugar bowl on my chest of drawers. The mother remarked that they looked like keys to a bike lock, and I had to admit she was right. They didn't ask about him. I said he could sit upright on the edge of the bed for nearly a minute. No need for the tube any more. I said it wasn't anyone's fault. Thanks, said the girl's father, we'll try the keys. I craned my neck to see the empty room behind them. The floor was covered with plastic and where M's bed used to stand, a work light cast its garish beam across the walls and ceiling.

Once he became more aware of where he was, and they let him make short trips outside the ward, we took the lift down to the foyer and I pushed him into the hospital chapel by way of experiment. A high-ceilinged room that smelled of resin. *Get me out*, he shouted, *get me out of here*. I took it as a good sign. He – unlike me – had always been an avowed atheist, and whenever we visited a church on our holidays, he would stay smoking in the sunshine while I let myself be sucked in, wandering aimlessly through the spongy silence that accumulates in places like that. That's how I want to remember him:

waiting in a strip of sunlight on the other side of the road, patient and proud and very, very beautiful.

I never stopped desiring him. Even after the baby came, love politely stayed nearby, and whenever we could we slipped away to be alone with it. His parents took care of our son while we went on long drives up the coast, where we'd turn off into a forest and do it among the trees or in the car. Our first night without the baby we stayed at a hotel in Granada. I remember the almond tart dusted with icing sugar, the fine rain that settled on my face as we wandered around the palace gardens.

On Christmas Eve I decided to let the child see him. Our son lit up and laughed at the sight of his father, but when M reached out for him and accidentally grabbed the boy's throat, I screamed so loudly that he began to cry. Taking the shrieking child to my parents outside, I told them I'd take the bus home, and that I'd be back in time for dinner. By the time I returned to the room, M had forgotten our visit. His short-term memory was in pieces, the minutes slipping through him like water. Nothing stuck. *Is that you?* he asked, and I said it was. When the tray of duck and sauce and potatoes arrived, I helped him lift the fork to his mouth, and I made sure he didn't drink so much squash that he threw up. The occupational therapist called his condition *non-critical*. His brain overlooked his body's satiety signals, but there was nothing to indicate that M was overeating. In the ten days since the accident, he'd lost so much muscle mass that his T-shirts were loose across his chest. When he was finished with the main, I peeled the lid off the plastic tub of rice pudding and put the spoon in his hand. *Can you manage?* I asked. He nodded. *Merry Christmas*, I said, kissing him goodbye. *I love you.* Say it again: *I love you.*

M did his rehab without complaint, and if there was a group singing session or a games night on the ward, he always took part. After a month at the hospital, he was covering short stretches on a walking frame and could recall for increasingly longer periods of time where he was and what he was doing there. *An accident*, he said hesitantly. *Did I have a car accident? A fall?* He treated his carers with a distant politeness and took pains not to get them confused. Dorthe, Louise, Gitte,Yvonne,Vibeke. I felt deep gratitude to the strong and gentle women who looked after him, and although they occasionally talked down to him, I couldn't blame them. There's something unmistakably childlike about a person who's hit their head. An innocence, or just a lasting wonder.

Gradually, as I came to know the patients on the ward, I arranged them in a hierarchy of presence. At the bottom were those who still hadn't left, and would probably never leave, their vegetative states. Kevin's mother watched enviously as I came trundling down the corridor with M. She sat by her son's bed and waited for him to cough. *It helps me remember his voice*, she said without self-pity. On the door of the wardrobe hung a picture of a young man with a broad face smiling shyly into the room. The driver coming the wrong way down the motorway had died at the scene; his two friends got away with scratches. Kevin's mother envied me, while I envied the relatives visiting patients with broken legs and bad hearts and infections – even cancer. Somewhere between Kevin at the bottom and M, who seemed to be able to do something new every day, was a group of people who couldn't get out of their wheelchairs but could make gestures. People whose communicative abilities were reduced to signals of disgust and enthusiasm, or whose facial expressions were wiped clean, everything hanging slack or tightened into a knot around the nose. The variations were endless and brutal. A Turkish man made a particular impression on me. He was more than six foot six and because he was non-critical like M, but didn't have M's metabolism, all his jumpers crept too short, gradually revealing a soft, hairy belly. The man travelled the ward's rectangular corridors in short steps, his gaze fixed on a point in the air ahead. His arms hung straight and his fingers were curved, as though he were asleep. The only time I saw him even remotely animated was when a physiotherapist offered him a cup of hot chocolate from the machine in the lounge. Then he grinned, drank it in three gulps and immediately asked for more. I was told later he'd worked at the vegetable market – an accident at work, it was – and I couldn't stop seeing the truck bed hammer down on the roof of his skull, transforming Mehmet there and then into a man-child whom his wife regarded with such immense helplessness I had to look away each time the family brought their food into the shared kitchen. The children had each other. They could hide in their own world, fight and play in the halls. She was irrevocably alone.

We got onto the 1A bus at Lille Triangel. I stopped short and tugged the snowsuit down over the child's tummy, taking off his elephant hat. We were outside the world. It was a simple time. I had no expectations of the days. The bus glided past the Citadel and along Store Kongensgade, past the shiny and expensive things, and at Magasin the tourists arrived in groups, before we wove through the city towards the main railway station. As the bus turns off Tietgen Bridge and continues down Ingerslevsgade, you get a few seconds' glimpse of our courtyard gate. After the accident I'd been back to the flat just once. The plan was to fetch books and clothes, make sure the lights and hobs were switched off, empty the fridge and take out the bins. My mother waited in the car, and I pressed my face into a T-shirt he'd worn. Longing enters the body like no other emotion. It swoops and spreads so fast you think you're about to cleave from head to toe. I stood in our bedroom and breathed through the threadbare cotton until the smell of him was indiscernible from the smell of the room. I pushed the wire drawer back into place with my foot and shut the wardrobe, made the bed. In the kitchen I washed up glasses and wiped down the table. I filled three IKEA bags with clothes and books.

The Friday it happened, M had left work early. He walked into the salon while I was still sitting with the heavy collar around my neck and the gown hanging from my shoulders. The hairdresser asked him to take a seat on the sofa behind me. I caught his eye in the mirror, feeling awkward about my new hair, which she wouldn't stop fiddling with. It hung down over my face in smooth hanks. There's a picture of me taken at a cafe where we went afterwards and which we left to go home and screw. I remember he took me from behind, but not if he came that way, or how I did. I took a picture of myself in the living room with PhotoBooth. You only see me from the neck up, but I know I'm naked, that he's in the bathroom as I'm sending it to my sister, writing: *new haircut!* I saw him for the last time on the landing. The black beanie, the coat. He could really thunder down a set of stairs. I closed the door and went back into the bedroom to get dressed – black turtleneck, high boots. I picked up the handbag he had given me in Granada. Blue and soft, it bulged with the packets of rice pudding, the freezer bag of blanched almonds and the cherry sauce I'd bought that morning. The rain was fierce, and I tucked the bag under my jacket to protect the leather.

It was still raining when I called him shortly after midnight, on my way home in a taxi. I could hear the party behind him, and he sounded cheerful and sober. His blood alcohol level is written down in the medical notes somewhere in a folder in his new apartment, but it doesn't matter any more. It makes no difference. I don't know if we said we loved each other, but why shouldn't we have said it?

THE GOLDEN LADY. MAI'S MASSAGE. THE FLOWER CORNER. At one point on the motorway it would feel like we were driving somewhere far away, before the bus reached its final stop and swung into a holding bay outside Hvidovre Hospital. The passengers had mostly thinned out by then, just a few of them getting off. Sometimes I was the only one. In the three months, when I made that trip each day, I noticed a certain type of man using the hospital foyer as a shelter. Perhaps they were homeless, perhaps just lonely. Or they simply preferred the crowd to the silence of their apartments. One brought a bag of rolls to eat in front of a television screen. Another, older and clubfooted, bought an orange soda and drank it at a table in the cafeteria. A few looked more down-at-heel, their hair greasy and matted. The men were always there when I arrived, and I never saw them take the bus home again, although of course they did.

For a long time after the accident, M couldn't remember our son's birth. The past came to him in flashes, and I did what I could to seize his islands of clarity, connect and extend them, hoping a coastal string of memories would emerge that corresponded to my own. I described in detail extracts from our life together. Our last fight, what we used to have for dinner, the pattern on our bedclothes, the routines of caring for our child. The series we were watching. After a while the question took on the character of an entreaty: *do you remember?*

It kept snowing well into spring. Gitte arranged for us to borrow a pram from Paediatrics, a moss-green Odder from the nineties with the number of the department written on the side in black pen. It made me uneasy to clip my son into the harness, as though the pram itself could make him sick. M and I took the lift down to the foyer and emerged from the swing doors. Cutting through the area where the buses turned around, we walked across the lawn between some residential blocks, crossed a single-lane road and went into the churchyard, where we wandered up and down the muddy paths. I felt a bottomless exhaustion. After a few laps I let him push the pram, but his gait was strange and stiff, and he dragged his feet. The sound woke the child, and I grabbed the pram in irritation and asked him to walk normally. *It's my shoes*, he said. *They're too big.* I told him the injuries had affected his balance. *It's because I'm not used to walking on anything except bamboo floors*, he muttered. *Smooth, shiny bamboo floors. No. That's not right. You hit your head, and you don't know what you're talking about. You're a patient at Hvidovre Hospital, right over there. See.* I pointed in the direction of the grey buildings, their flat roofs peeping from behind a row of black trees. He squinted, the hat concealing the fact that his hair had grown too long and stuck out boyishly around his ears. I had to be kinder to him, and more patient. One day he'd look at the world again as though it belonged to him – at me, as though I did. I smiled and slipped my arm into his. The hope was euphoric, and it lifted me up and made me strong, until it dropped me again with a suddenness that took my breath away. In that state it took everything I had to cling on and stay lifted.

At the end of March we were called in for a meeting to discuss discharging M. The sun was shining, and there was an expectant mood around the table. I sat at the head (we were the guests of honour) next to M, who had a calendar open in front of him. He wrote in capitals like before, but the letters were big and childishly tilted, as though pulled by a magnet in the bottom right-hand corner. The neuropsychologist spoke first, then the rest of the team took turns. By this point M had taken the bus into the city and visited the apartment twice. Last time, as part of the discharge process, he did the shopping and made an omelette with Manchego and asparagus. After watching him cook, the occupational therapist packed up her things and left us. We ate the omelette in the cold, because the radiators had been off all winter. Cutting it in half, he laid a piece on my plate. It was tasty, and we ate all of it. I longed desperately to be outside my body, like you do sometimes when you've got food poisoning or an upcoming exam. The illness that seemed almost natural at the hospital was impossible to ignore now that he was back at the apartment. We ate in silence, wearing our jackets. I smiled encouragingly at him. He had deeply and utterly changed for me.

Waking up is just starting the loss again from the beginning, only worse.

A few months after the accident, I found a CD-ROM with some grainy footage of him from before we had met. In the video M is the same age as I am now. Wearing a checked tweed hat, obviously high. He and a friend have built a makeshift catapult onto which, gingerly, he places a hand-rolled cigarette. Pausing for effect, he brings his fist down like a hammer onto one end of the ruler, and the cigarette flies up past his snapping jaws and lands on the floor. He mugs for the camera anyway, an agile look on his face, as though he'd actually managed to grab it. He keeps up the self-assured grimace for a few seconds before cracking into laughter, and the friend behind the camera does the same. Then it finishes. I don't have the courage to watch it again, because there you are, and I can't bear it, and I don't even want to try.

This unspeakable shame: to contain not a single sentence worthy of you.

I'm lying.

Your name. Say it. ■

Ken Babstock

Tasked with Designing the Vienna House

After a wet spring, the rattan mat
that spent May caught in a maple
looks like hair, a note of horror
on a cul-de-sac, blowing out kinks
under lamplight. The modest row
of semi-detached homes pull
their blinds at my tower block,
making a good show of being
put upon, poor things, their
petunias. Sky of bright rust and
soapy aquamarine. A half lemon
wrinkles, extrudes slick seeds
and the flies appear. I don't know
how I do it. How the city does it,
constantly appearing as paper,

collaged and aswim in emulsion,
then tipping over into dystopia,
white cell count of the expressway,
the cellophane chill, the organic
chicken. I love graffiti for being
a constant among the variables.
Least aware when I need milk
for the morning, the unplanned

script is everywhere its own fiat
and mark of lives asking I license
some unseen assembly. In one
version of living a non-viable midlife
under the present aesthetic, I'm
to *reach people*, I take it, my laser
pointer, my pager, though the last

I saw of them they waved happily
from a quayside bar in Rotterdam,
glad to know I was away safe, or
away, and would damage no more
of de Kooning's mom's hotel.
Europe's like that, awash in names
and hard drugs. In Rotterdam I sat
in a very narrow folding seat while
Tranströmer played 'Piano Concerto
for the Left Hand' which Ravel
had written for Wittgenstein's brother
who'd lost his right hand in the war.
A vessel bursts in my right eye.
A vessel leaves port bound for my
right eye. Imagine the right feelings.

Untitled, 2013
Galerie Taménaga

ON BEING FRENCH
AND CHINESE

Tash Aw

On 7 August 2016, Zhang Chaolin, a forty-nine-year-old tailor, was savagely beaten by a group of youths in Aubervilliers, a deprived suburb on the northern outskirts of Paris – the latest in a string of violent aggressions against ethnic Chinese. Like the other victims, he had been targeted because of the widely held belief that members of the Chinese community habitually carry large amounts of cash (and that they are docile and unlikely to fight back; that they are reluctant to report crimes because they are in the country illegally, or cannot express themselves properly in French; and even if they do, the police do not take them seriously; or, simply, that the Chinese 'keep themselves to themselves'). As it turned out, Zhang Chaolin only had a packet of cigarettes and some sweets on him. He died as a result of his injuries five days later.

The following year, on 26 March, fifty-six-year-old Liu Shaoyo was preparing dinner for his children in his apartment in the 19th arrondissement in Paris when the police arrived at his home following a call from neighbours (the nature of the complaint remains unclear). The precise sequence of events is disputed: his family insist firmly that he had merely been gutting fish and had answered the door while still holding a pair of kitchen scissors; the police claim that they had acted in self-defence. Either way, they opened fire, killing Liu Shaoyo.

In the aftermath of each man's death, huge demonstrations were held by France's ethnic Chinese, a community traditionally invisible in national discourse and under-represented in public life. I was transfixed by video footage of a crowd of over 15,000 in the Place de la République in 2016 shortly after Chaolin's death on 12 August, protesting against continuing attacks on ethnic Chinese in Paris. Much of what I heard in the speeches that day, as well as in newspaper reports and on social media, felt tragically familiar to me: the cries of a people who felt that they had been ignored by the state. *We work hard, we keep out of trouble, no one gives a damn about us, we have to struggle all by ourselves.* These were the sentiments I grew up with in my ethnic Chinese family in Malaysia – a sense of frustration and suppressed pain that informed my view of the world.

But there was also something totally foreign to me about these protests: the open dissent. Pushing back against hierarchy and authority. The protesters were overwhelmingly young, incredibly vocal and, in some instances, willing to resort to violent action – the very opposite of how overseas Chinese communities, the centuries-old immigrants known as huaqiao – have traditionally behaved. In short, the demonstrations seemed to be distinctly French.

I had been as surprised as most people to learn that France has the largest ethnic-Chinese population in Europe. In a country where race-based statistics sit uneasily with the notion of *égalité* and French citizenship, it's often difficult to find accurate figures, though most estimates suggest a population of at least 600,000–700,000, more than double that of the United Kingdom.

There were other surprises too. In France, where I have travelled and lived on and off for more than fifteen years, I have always taken the French habit of calling anyone of East or South East Asian appearance '*chinois*' as a laziness bordering on casual racism, particularly since France is home to large Vietnamese and Cambodian communities who arrived in the country in great numbers following the wars in the former French colonies in the 1970s. But as I got to know members of the various Asian communities in Paris, I discovered that I had been guilty of overlooking a fact that should have been obvious to me, of all people: that the overwhelming majority of Cambodians and Vietnamese in France are of Chinese descent. That is to say, like me, they come from South East Asian Chinese families – families who had already been immigrants in their home countries before moving to Europe, and for whom being an outsider is integral to their sense of identity. Their languages – Cantonese and Teochew – are those I have lived with my whole life.

I learned, too, of the vast distinctions within the Chinese community, principally between the South East Asians and the huge numbers of newer immigrants from the mainland, overwhelmingly from the factory-port city of Wenzhou.

I met the people who had organised the most visible of the demonstrations. They have since mobilised themselves into a group that promotes not just political but social and cultural change – the Association of Young Chinese of France, one of the most notable of the many Asian action groups that are being established in the country. Over the course of many months, we've walked through the Asian neighbourhoods of Paris, shared meals and become friends over the messy issue of mixed identity. They've spoken about what it means to be French and Chinese.

93: Crossroads

The suburbs of Aubervilliers and Pantin lie just beyond the north-eastern corner of the périphérique, part of the département of Seine-Saint-Denis, notorious in the French public imagination for its perceived levels of crime and deprivation, and known colloquially as 'le neuf-trois' after its departmental number. At Quatre Chemins, the crossroads that form the heart of the neighbourhood, the first building I see when I emerge from the Métro bears a sign that reads HÔTEL À LA JOURNÉE/€53 LA NUIT. People hurry along the streets, as if to and from work, in contrast to the more bourgeois districts of Paris, which are already empty now that the summer holidays are here.

Rui, age thirty-two:

'I arrived in France in 1995, when I was seven and a half. My parents had already been here for some years, having arrived in Europe from Wenzhou, in the south of China. They had papers for Italy but had come to France illegally, so when I arrived I was an illegal too. One of my earliest memories of my childhood in France was of my father not returning home one night, and my mother telling me that he'd been arrested by the police for not having the right papers. He didn't come home for three days. Eventually he was released – they couldn't prove anything, so he was free to come home, but we lived with that fear all the time. It was exhausting.

'Before we got our papers, I lived constantly with my father's shame – the shame of being a poor clandestine. We lived entirely within the Chinese community, that is to say, entirely within the Wenzhou community. Some had papers, many didn't. There was a very distinct hierarchy, a division between those who were legal and those who weren't. In those early days, not so many of us had a passport, and if you got married to a French citizen it was like getting married to Bill Gates or Hillary Clinton – the most privileged thing in the world!

'My father was the opposite end of this spectrum. He worked in the lowest of shitty jobs, as a *plongeur* in Chinese restaurants – that sort of thing. I could feel his shame at being an illegal immigrant every time he talked to anyone. I could hear it in his voice – he felt crushed by the world. *Why?* I asked myself. Why do we have to live with this shame? I would go home at night and cry myself to sleep. Because they were illegals, my parents were forced to accept their position at the bottom of the ladder, and their inferiority complex coloured my experience of life, even at that age.

'Every single time they went out, my parents would take me along with them. "In France the police won't arrest us if we have a child with us," they used to say. Even at that age, I knew that I was being used as a human shield. I'd be playing or reading quietly at home and suddenly my parents would say, "We need to go out." I never had any time for myself. Sometimes I feel as though I had my childhood taken away from me, confiscated against my will.

'People don't stay in Quatre Chemins long. As soon as they have a decent job and some money, they move to a better neighbourhood. Those who stay aren't so lucky. We were here for many years, just up the road on the Pantin side of the crossroads. Down there, just a couple of hundred metres away, was where Zhang Chaolin was attacked. There's been a lot of talk in recent years about the violence in Aubervilliers and Pantin, but in truth it's always been difficult here, there's always been aggressions, robberies, fights. [*As if on cue, at our very first meeting in a cafe in the heart of Quatre Chemins, a fight suddenly breaks out between the Wenzhounese cafe owner and a man who had walked in off the street, an altercation which spills out onto the pavement and results in the appearance of the police in just a few minutes.*] This is where the Chinese community live, but they mostly work on the other side of Aubervilliers, where they run wholesale businesses, mainly of clothes, shoes and bags. It's a barren area, very harsh, and it's on the way to and from work that they've been getting attacked and robbed. What you hear about Chinese people feeling scared and not wanting to go out unless they're in groups – it's true. But look around you: you can see we also have ordinary lives in a very mixed community.

'It looked as if our lives were condemned to forever being lived in the shadows, and my parents were ready to abandon their French dream and return to Italy. But then, in 1997 a *coup de théâtre*, and suddenly our fortunes were transformed. Jacques Chirac, who was president at the time, decided to call fresh legislative elections because he believed they would reinforce the right and destroy the left. But the plan backfired and instead it was the left who won the elections and proceeded to put in place a programme of regularisation for people who'd lived without papers for many years in the country. All of a sudden, we became normal members of society, and that changed everything for us: the kinds of jobs my parents were suddenly eligible for, the way they could hold their heads up in public, even my behaviour at school. I felt confident, I felt the same as everyone else. It's not as if we became rich or anything, but almost overnight, we felt as if life held possibilities for us. I remember the day we got our papers, my mother took me to a restaurant for the first time – a simple Vietnamese place where we had pho. It felt like such a luxury.

'Now that I have a good job – I work in real estate, I have a decent income and I own a nice apartment – I sometimes think back to those days of poverty, when we were illegal and my family had no money, no possibility of earning money or of getting any social security. And I realise that a large part of the shame was what we were going to tell our family back in China. We had left to build better lives for ourselves in France, but here we were, worse off than before. We were trapped in a sort of double prison: by poverty in Europe, and by China and its expectations of us.

'After I became a full French citizen at the age of eighteen, I started to think more deeply about my identity – about what it meant to be French, and also Chinese. By that time, I and all my cousins and friends, people who'd been brought up or even born in France, had experienced racism in France – from casual insults, people mocking our accents, or more serious incidents like being robbed because we were seen as weak and docile. And then, during the Beijing Olympics, we saw how the French media talked about China and *the Chinese*, as if we were one kind of people, who acted in the same way, always in the image of the Communist Party. That got me really mad, so together with other friends like me – young Chinese people who considered France their only home – I formed the Association of Young Chinese of France. I was at university at the time, at Paris Dauphine, and reading Marx and Bourdieu – people who helped me make sense of my childhood, of the way my parents' experience conditioned mine. I wanted to change things – for me and also for them.

'When Zhang Chaolin was in hospital and everyone knew he was going to die, I knew I had to do something. Together with a few other young people, we made plans for a huge demonstration that we would put into action the moment he died. When I saw all those people gathered for the demonstration outside the mairie of the 19th arrondissement, I felt elated – as if change was finally happening.

'What happened at the demonstration to mark Liu Shaoyo's death was even more remarkable. The elders of the Chinese community had organised a formal event, full of boring speeches that tried to appease everyone. Everything was expressed in neutral language, with typical Chinese politesse. Not that many people were present. Then, not long before proceedings were due to wrap up, a huge swathe of protesters dressed in black descended towards the Place de la République, shouting slogans against the establishment. All of them were young Chinese people, angry with the inaction of the older generation. They wanted change, they wanted it urgently. All of it was calculated to make the elders lose face, to show how powerless and pointless they were. It was exhilarating to see that mass of young people trying to wrest control from their elders.

'For me, the demonstrations were a form of revenge. For the humiliation that my parents experienced. That I've experienced. The humiliation of being rendered invisible, of not being listened to. The humiliation that Chinese people go through every time they are aggressed in the street, which is a continuation of the marginalisation my parents lived through.

'But above all, these protests, this spirit of revolution – this is what makes me French. In Chinese culture, as you and I both know all too well, we're trained to be obedient, to respect your elders and hierarchy in general. In France it's the reverse. You became integrated from the moment you feel able to criticise, especially if you criticise the state and the government. It's a particularly French quality, almost a disease, I would say! In this country, we are French, we are required to be French, and this requires a very special mentality. For Chinese-French people, it's not the same as Chinese-Italians or Chinese-Spanish, who are always thinking they will never be fully integrated and will probably go back to China in ten years' time. We think of our children and grandchildren living normal lives in this country, so we need to change things. I have a way of thinking which I feel defines a French person: I believe that the government can always, *always*, be changed. I believe in the power of revolution to change our lives.'

13: South East Asia

T*he southern end of Paris's 13th arrondissement is home to the city's largest and longest-established Asian community, composed principally of families who fled the civil wars in Cambodia, Vietnam and Laos, arriving in France in large numbers after the fall of Saigon and Phnom Penh in 1975. The heart of Chinatown is concentrated around the famous residential towers blocks known as Les Olympiades, completed in the mid-1970s – the first homes to be occupied by the families arriving from South East Asia.*

Laëtitia, age twenty-five:

'One of the things my parents often used to say in reprimanding me was "*Tu es devenue trop Française*" – you've become too French. Whenever they were angry they also used the term "*ang mo kia*", which was not intended as a compliment ['*white kid*' *in many of the dialects of southern China, shorthand for rude, rebellious behaviour, Western values being of course the antithesis of harmony, both within the family and in society*]. I think it came from a frustration that we, their children, had very little idea of what they went through so that we could grow up with an idea of being French, and only French. But then again, they never spoke of their lives before coming to France, or their difficult journeys here, so it's no surprise that most of us only have a single French identity.

'My parents are Sino-Cambodian, that is to say, ethnic Chinese Teochews from Chaozhou who were born or grew up in Cambodia with a dual identity, both Chinese and Cambodian. During the war, just before the country fell to the Khmer Rouge, they were forced to flee, abandoning everything they had and, in some cases, even members of their own family. They spent the whole of the war trapped in camps on the Thai border. During that time, who knows what kind of horrors they witnessed? I can understand why they wouldn't want to talk about it. Like many Cambodians, their lives had been all right over there – they ran shops and small businesses. Then, almost overnight: the war, the nightmare of departure, and finally France.

'Despite my parents' silence, I knew that they survived unspeakable brutality in Cambodia, and this knowledge is something unspoken that I carry within me, affecting the way I feel about France. Intellectually, I can understand why the *gilets jaunes* are protesting, I'm French after all, I have the tendency to question the way other French people do. But when you know that your parents have survived one of the greatest genocides the world has ever seen, everything becomes relative. When people talk of *life's great problems* being the price of petrol and only being able to go to a restaurant once a week, or only having one holiday a year, we can't feel fully invested in these arguments even if we understand them. My parents ran a restaurant when I was a child, and I can't remember them ever taking a holiday. That's why they pushed me to have a life where I could make choices and have greater agency than them.

'As a rule, I don't think you'll find many French people from South East Asian Chinese families, that is to say Cambodian or Vietnamese, who are passionate about the right to take to the streets. We don't take the attitude that "the government has to do everything for me". Even back in Cambodia and Vietnam, our families were already outsiders. We didn't benefit from any structural help then, we didn't come from the dominant class in those countries, we didn't feel we had the right to demand anything. We knew we had to fend for ourselves. Even though the overwhelming majority of Asians of my generation would consider themselves French and only French, I don't know anyone who relies on state subsidies to live – two generations of French citizenship are not enough to change the embedded mentality of self-sufficiency.

'French identity is an incredibly powerful idea. Being French is a notion that is inculcated within us from the earliest days at primary school, and it's a really attractive principle: a project of assimilation to push aside cultural origins to create one single nationality, one people. But the problem is that differences persist, and as my teenage years went by I suddenly began to think there's something missing, some part of myself that is not acknowledged, and that's when I began to interrogate the Chinese part of myself, and learn how to be culturally Chinese as well as French.

'You can see the problems in the unacknowledged differences in culture and race when you look at the aggression against Chinese people in certain parts of Paris. Asian and North African communities live in tough conditions and have come to think about each other in negative stereotypes. We can't speak about it along racial lines because to do so is taboo, totally contrary to the ideas of the republic, of *égalité* and so on. But the problems exist.

'The rise of China has been complicated for us. Before that, no one really noticed Asian people – we just got on with our lives in a nearly invisible way. Then I began to hear overtly racist comments like, *Chinese spit everywhere, they're filthy, they're money launderers*. The most negative phase was in 2008–9, during the Beijing Olympics, when suddenly the old "Yellow Peril" fears were everywhere. All the time, we had newspaper stories entitled CHINA: CONQUERING THE WORLD. There were TV programmes like *Envoyé Special*, which killed Chinese delicatessens almost overnight by screening "exposés" on hygiene standards. My parents ran one of those delis, so I should know.

'I guess that's why many people from my community say that they are Cambodian, or Vietnamese, to distance themselves from associations with the mainland, and from the newer immigrants from Wenzhou, who've only been in France for twenty years or so. We've been here since the 1970s, and already, there's a sense within our communities of being more French than they are, more part of the community, which gives us a sense of superiority. The things we say about them echo what the rest of France say about us: that they work really hard, they're prepared to work very long hours for next to nothing, they keep themselves to themselves, and so on. We're used to being the model immigrants, but there are newer versions of ourselves, and we pass judgements on them. Maybe that's a sign of belonging to French society.'

Daniel, age twenty-seven:

'I would say that among all my Asian friends, I'm in the minority of those who are comfortable with being both Asian and French. A very small number, I guess those who've been victims of consistent racism, choose to reject their French identity, but the vast majority are more comfortable inhabiting only a French identity and are prepared to reject any sense of Asian-ness if it clashes with feeling French.

'From what I see in my circle of friends, ethnic Chinese are far more likely to reject their Chinese-ness than a *Maghrebin* their Arab-ness. I'm not sure why – maybe it's to do with the silence that exists within many families, particularly those from Vietnam and Cambodia, the lack of knowledge about our histories. We're not connected to our non-French past the way Arabs and Africans are. They tend to have extended families back in Côte d'Ivoire or Morocco or Algeria who provide them with a link to their cultures, their languages. We don't have that – there's no one back in Vietnam who can give me that sense of belonging to another culture. In any case, there's a complication, because my family are ethnic Chinese who speak Cantonese, so which is my "other" culture?

'There's a question of visibility too. Black Africans and North Africans are represented in public life – in sports, music and pop culture in general – whereas we are almost totally absent. That means that it's more difficult for us to identify role models.

'Another pressure is that our parents often live life through us. Their aspirations, all the things they weren't able to achieve because they arrived in France too late in life, traumatised and with very little money, they invest in us. Part of that means figuring out how to live in France. Many of us have experience of being interpreters for our parents even when we were very small. So of course it's natural we end up behaving like models of French society.

'We don't recognise ourselves in French history, which is one of the most important subjects at school, because this is a country that has a long and rich history. We absorb all the lessons on French heroes such as Jeanne d'Arc, Charlemagne, Clovis. It's one single version of history, one story, which everyone, even children of immigrant families are obliged to accept as their own. Even though I tried to feel that it was my story, I couldn't help feeling a bit detached from it. To accept that version of history as my only heritage felt false – it was a story that rendered us invisible. Coupled with the misleading stereotypes elsewhere, it felt to me that our fate in society was either not to be talked about, or to be talked about inaccurately.

'We were taught next to nothing about Vietnam, which was after all one of France's most important colonies for a hundred years. Colonial history – France's relationship with countries that would provide large numbers of its minority populations – wasn't taught much at school, which was a shame. I remember the kids of Algerian origin being very interested in lessons on the war in Algeria. They felt as if it spoke of them, that the whole class was learning about them and their past, where their parents came from, why they were French, how they were French. There was nothing for us, but in some ways that's natural. Algeria represents a greater presence in the French imagination than Vietnam, even if that relationship is problematic. You have to understand, we grow up with the notion that all of us are French – that is the whole point of our history lessons, to give us one single shared identity. I get that. But isn't it more important to learn why we are so diverse? We're all French, but these days there are so many different ways of being French. I'd have loved to have learned more about the histories of the different communities in France – their music, art, language. I'd also have liked to learn about the history of racism, rather than have to figure it all out myself.'

11: Gentrification

B *oulevard Voltaire is just a fifteen-minute walk from the Place de la Bastille and its concentration of hip bars and restaurants, yet it feels much more down at heel. Most of the shops sell clothing but there are no customers in them; they have names like Veti Style, Lucky Men and Bella. Many other shop lots are closed and available to rent.*

Emma, age nineteen:

'Until I was in my mid-teens, I never had any Chinese friends. In fact I made a point not to hang out with other Chinese kids. I only had white, Arab or black friends – I was born here and wanted to show how French I was. But around sixteen, seventeen, I started to change. I'd had conversations with my parents, who'd come to France from Wenzhou when they were young. "No matter how you feel inside," my father told me, "when the world looks at you, they see a Chinese person." It was around that time too that I began to realise that all the things I'd accepted as normal – people mocking Chinese accents to my face, even though I speak just like any other French person, casual comments sexualising Asian women and desexualising Asian men – were micro-aggressions, and that I had to embrace my culture, instead of reject it.

'My parents ran a *bar-tabac* towards the Oberkampf side of the 11th arrondisement. I wanted to do what bourgeois white French kids do, so I applied to Sciences Po, one of the most prestigious of the country's *grandes écoles*. Few people in my community thought it was worth it – they couldn't imagine it possible for me to pursue a career in human or social sciences, and definitely not in politics. There aren't any statistics on how many Asians there are at Sciences Po, but just from my own observations, there are fewer than ten per year, which means thirty in the entire school. It's not like in the US, where Asians are a very visible presence on every major college campus – our elite schools still feel quite foreign to us. Maybe in the more science-based schools there might be more Asians, but personally I really don't know any. If you look at schools like École normale supérieure, which require you to have amassed great cultural knowledge by the time you're eighteen or twenty, the figure is probably zero.

'Whatever the real situation, the general impression within the Chinese community is that the most exclusive schools are bastions that we'd have difficulty gaining access to, so when I got in, it was a really, really big achievement. Things are changing now, but not as fast as you'd imagine. In the French imagination, Asians are studious and conscientious, but if that were true, we would be much more visible in the *grandes écoles*, which are, after all, the standard bearers of French education.' ■

'Jupiter's magnetic field is fragilising its moon Europa'
– Arnaud Sacleux, *National Geographic* headline, 2019

Europa, a satellite of Jupiter, is covered by an ocean buried beneath an enormous shell of ice. Its surface is magnificent, like hammered pewter, striated with lines, bumpy with domes and pierced by geysers. Jupiter's fluctuating magnetic field creates tides that threaten the physical cohesion of Europa. Its surface is fissuring, and plumes of water shoot out into space. It is cold on Europa but this water, this core, well protected from solar radiation, strongly suggests the possibility of life: both for us, as a Planet B, and for the moon itself. These creatures on Europa might resemble those that live in the depths of our terrestrial oceans, in the sulphurous frigidity of night.

The very large planet and the tiny little satellite make me think of the immensity of the death drive and the stubbornness of the life drive. There is a Europe of life and a Europe of death, on the mass graves of which we perpetuate a dream. A Europe of bloodstained snow, and a Europe of sublime forests, valleys and cities. The Treaty of Versailles was signed amid the beauty of such stones exactly one hundred years ago. The fetishism of borders, the rancour and narcissism remain. The certainty that one may possess an identity as if it were a horse or a car, and a country as if it were a woman, remains. The personality cult of the leader, the economic greed and fatalism remain, only slightly displaced by contemporary fields of attraction and the massive proliferation of commentaries.

The space probe *Voyager* recorded the sounds of Europa: a steady shrill crunching with bubbles, small singing voices, and growls. ∎

Translated from the French by Linda Coverdale

Andrew Miller, 1979
Courtesy of the author

ITINERANT

Andrew Miller

I signed up to work as a cleaner at Schiphol airport but the job wouldn't start for another ten days and in the meantime I would have to manage on what I had, which was two weeks' UK dole money, in 1979 something just shy of fifty pounds.

I stayed in the Amsterdam city hostel, the Sleep-Inn, for which I paid at the door six guilders a night (in advance). It was an old industrial building and we slept on rolls of yellow foam, each side of each large, bare room, one continuous roll. A cool and stony light in there, people's sleeping bags and rucksacks weighing down those lolling yellow tongues. All through the night the soft (mostly soft) coming and going of others.

On the ground floor there was a common area in the style of a student union. I don't remember much light ever getting into it. At the bar they sold a beer named after the river and perhaps containing the river, and it might have been at the Sleep-Inn I first saw that neat way of pouring beer into small glasses then slicing off the head of foam with a piece of plastic like a flattened shoehorn. And there was food too, the kind you sell in semi-darkness to young people – toasted sandwiches, frites, types of sausage. Nothing cost much; no one had much. That was the point of it, a way, a building, to collect up the boys and girls who would otherwise find shop doorways for themselves or bed down in the corridors of the central railway station. Amsterdam had had years of it. Old Pathé films from the 1960s show the wavy-haired in-search-of-fun youth (many from Britain) sleeping head to toe in Dam Square. The Sleep-Inn – a tram ride from the centre – tidied us up as the city grew a little weary of having to step over other people's slack-eyed children as it went about its day.

And by '79, things were changing. There were punks on the streets and the Summer of Love was a fading memory. In March, the year I arrived, the IRA shot dead the British Ambassador to the Netherlands. A year earlier, in Rome, Aldo Moro's murdered body was left in the boot of a car. Thatcher was in power; Reagan soon to be. The Cold War was turning away from detente, watchers East and West tensed over their radar screens.

Did they play punk at the Sleep-Inn? At the Melkweg and the Paradiso nightclubs that year, XTC and the B-52s played gigs, Siouxsie and the Banshees, the Cure, the Buzzcocks. But at the Sleep-Inn I think disco still held its ground, just. Donna Summer, Boney M, Sister Sledge. 'We Are Family' was the hit of the summer and they played it again and again through the big speakers above the bar.

My first morning at the Sleep-Inn, waking late, I took my towel through to the washrooms at the rear of the building. One of the showers was already in use, and in the cubicle, under the showerhead, the rose, a black girl was soaping herself. I stopped, briefly electrified by the thought I had wondered into a forbidden zone, but it was the same utilitarian space I had cleaned my teeth in the night before. Nor did she shout at me (in whatever language she had) or turn away, Artemis disturbed by Actaeon. Instead, she regarded me with a degree of comfortable indifference that made it clear we were both where we were entitled to be. I looked – a second's worth of concentrated gazing – then the clumsy miming of a boundless interest in anything but her, a black girl lit by high windows, the Amsterdam sky played through coils of steam.

The world I had come from was one that might have been defined as somewhere unisex shower blocks *could not exist*. If they did, it could only have been as a type of pornography, or something louche, aristocratic, probably criminal. Here? I didn't know, I wasn't sure. What did it mean that a girl could wash herself in the same space as a boy, could be looked at but feel no awkwardness? This, perhaps, was what I'd come for, sitting eight hours on the vomit-scented ferry out of Harwich, the North Sea that can never be mistaken for friendly. To enter the liberal world of freely showering black girls! And if it was sexual – I was nineteen, everything was sexual – it was also just the thrumming-in of experience, an encounter, one of my first, with the erotic as a true medium of the imagination rather than a keyhole in a peep show. (Weeks later I went to a peep show in the red-light district, perhaps hoping to be reacquainted with shame, but even there found something plainer and more interesting, more human and broad-spectrum, hard to explain in an old Calvinist city.)

Getting work was not difficult. Little employment offices could be found on a dozen streets in the city centre. You filled out a form, showed your passport. The lack of any useful skills wasn't an impediment: there were plenty of jobs for people who were sound of limb, could pick things up and put them down, understand simple commands. The agency took a cut but it wasn't outrageous and it meant I could stay. My cleaning job at Schiphol sounded almost exciting. I just needed to navigate the time in between: the days before it started, then the first week of work before I was paid. I economised, after a fashion, fare-dodged on the yellow trams, had breakfast in the plainest cafes. Lunch was coffee and a roll-up, and for the evenings I relied on that key resource of the indigent, the Chinese restaurant, most especially the ones that were *upstairs*. I don't know why they should be cheaper, but they were. Something to do with the rent.

I did not entirely deny myself beer and certainly I was not without tobacco. I may also have bought a bag of grass at Laurier 33, a place I discovered on my second or third day in the city, a modest sort of establishment close to the Sleep-Inn that served good coffee, good cakes, and where a dozen different types of grass or resin were displayed for sale in clear plastic snap-bags. The business of buying it, so different to what I was used to – the furtive hook-up in the pub, then retiring with the dealer to the pub toilets or the darkest corner of the car park – confused me at first. What, choosing my little bag, was the correct degree of cool? How not to look what I was, new to it, wildly pleased, wanting to laugh? You could buy it, buy your coffee and get stoned right there, yet no one was lying on the floor or looking dangerous. It was another angle of the unisex showers thing, a depth of mellow that made England seem untutored, a slightly savage place watched over by an establishment that didn't really want people – ordinary people – to have too much fun, get too relaxed.

And so, slightly sooner than it needed to, the day came when I dug the last guilder out of my pocket, spent it and possessed nothing but the beginnings of an appetite I had no obvious way of appeasing. Cities are not friendly places to those who have nothing, but there must be degrees of unfriendliness and Amsterdam did not immediately threaten as other places might have done – London, for example. It was early June, the weather was kind. I walked the canal-sides, saw in murky green water the reflections of tall houses, those effusions of a Golden Age, grand in their way yet domestic too, a plainness like that of a good suit of dark clothes, the sort you could do business in at the Bourse then sit in the water-light of the Zuiderkerk speaking to God in that nice sticks-and-stones language I never learned more than a few words of the whole time I was there.

I was the young man in Knut Hamsun's *Hunger,* soul polished by poverty, not pegged down by the petty transactions, the money-life of the others. Such thoughts, rich in feeling, sustained me for several hours, particularly while I still had tobacco left. I squeezed poetry from the old streets, grew lighter in the head, lighter everywhere, a sallying-out of the spirit that lasted until I woke on the foam rubber tongue, aware not of soul but of belly, a hunger that roused in me – slacker boy, art boy – a lean and determined hunter.

In the quarter-light of very early I packed my rucksack and set out into the city. I did not have a plan but I had an appetite and it led me –

the compass of need – towards a market, thirty or so stalls spanning a bridge and the sides of a canal, and already at that hour full of bustle. How to begin? Would I steal? I could hardly hope, pack on my back, to outrun an enraged stallholder. Beg? I was still several rungs from that. So, something less brazen. I would scavenge, scrounge, become a gleaner, one of those (all antennae and jaws) that tidies up, living on the waste and spillings of others.

This was a prosperous market for people who had little interest in the bruised, the overripe. What was spoiled was discarded and lay on the cobbles in dabs of colour among the wooden crates. I took a pair of oranges, pulpy but serviceable. I like to think there may also have been a banana from some former Dutch colony – Aruba, Tobago, Tangasseri – but I can't remember. No one shouted; no one cared. If they saw me, well, they had seen it before and they had work to do. I moved down the canal, found a bench and made my breakfast.

Having, for the moment, solved the puzzle of hunger, I was ready to start on the puzzle of money. It does not take long when thinking of money to start thinking of banks. I had some idea the Dutch had invented them, or that they had, at least, been in there early. Their banks might be particularly flush. Serious money, old money, bundles of it, the oldest stuff like squares of tapestry, slightly damp from sitting so long in cellars bordered by water. And I needed so little! They might insist on more. They might – for what did I know of the emotions of banks? – be moved by such a modest request, strangely humbled. Anyway, I would go to a bank and I would reason with them. This would work.

I shouldered my pack and moved deeper into the city, the tightening whorl of water and stone. I was as exhilarated as a person can be who has breakfasted on oranges. I studied the banks I passed with what I imagined was a canny eye. Not too grand (I'd never get through the doors), not too specialised or unreadable, and certainly not with an armed guard outside, some portly faux-sheriff with a Village People moustache who might stare me down before I could make my entrance. At last I saw one that struck me as almost welcoming. I went in and approached the counter. The teller did not look alarmed, or not very. I started to explain. I had a job but it had not yet started. Soon (play up the positives, *stress* this) I would have a regular income. In the meantime I was in need of a small loan and, as security, I would offer not just my passport (here) but also my watch (a Timex, mid-range). The teller was young though not, of course, as young as I was. Very likely he had not dealt with this before, penniless foreigners offering their watches. A more senior man was summoned and I went through my pitch a second time, more fluently now though with a steady seeping away of confidence. The older man waited politely – they are a polite people, unexcitable – then gently pushed my passport back across the counter and shook his head.

I tried at least one more before I understood it, the way of the world, of banking, how money must have something to connect to (ideally, other money) and has no possible interest in young men who claim they will shortly have a job at an airport (no, not air traffic control or piloting a jet, but doing a little cleaning). It was nice no one had laughed at me or called the police.

I spent the night, the first in a series, in one of the city parks. I went in at dusk, moved towards a stand of trees, loitered there a moment as if taking in the summer sweetness, the park's soft outbreath of day, then stepped backwards, entered the treeline and hid. At some time in the small hours I was woken by the light of a torch, one end of the beam in my face, the other in the hand of a policeman. There were two of them. No doubt it was just a routine sweep. They were not angry or officious or threatening. They stood over me while I packed my sleeping bag then walked me to the park gates. For the length of a street I felt like a cat caught napping on a bed and sent, without ceremony, out the door. Wounded pride, twitching tail. A determination to appear, to whoever might be watching, to have chosen my fate. But then came the novelty of being out in the middle of the night in a city still mostly strange to me, a wanderer between shuttered houses and hushed streets. The unnoticed-by-day caught my eye now – the lazy scribble of tram lines, black flowers stiff in a window box, a bicycle abandoned but alert against a wall. I turned away from districts that looked more brightly lit or where taxis and police cars crossed at junctions. It was hard to know how serious it was, my being out there without even the money to make a phone call. Was this an adventure or was I in trouble? At what point did one begin to shade into the other?

Two hours of this, raw with tiredness (that state where you are both as heavy as the street you walk on and light as dust), I found what I needed. A quiet square, a scrap of green, a pair of trees, an old globe-headed street lamp like a finger hole poked through the tissue of night. And between the trees a wood and iron bench where I sat, then stretched out on, lowering myself past watchfulness and into the keeping of some dryad of the small squares whose face was hidden, whose nature was hidden.

In the morning, before I was seen, approached, questioned, I was gone.

The job at the airport was with a company called Q Service. The employees – or those who did the actual cleaning – wore overalls with a Q stitched over the left breast. We were collected from the city in a minibus and driven out to Schiphol, ten of us, sometimes twelve, squeezed into a dark green Spacevan. Even in the short time I worked for Q Service, the faces changed. No one was expected to stay for long. You worked, and when you judged you'd had enough, had filled out the shrunken belly of your wallet with sweetie-coloured banknotes – Frans Hals and a lovely blue for the 10; Jan Pieterszoon Sweelinck and the red of hope for the 25 – you quit.

As far as I could tell, no two of us came from the same country, and from the beginning the person I sat with on the bus, who I spoke to and who, now and then, I met outside of work, was a Swiss man I thought of as middle-aged, which probably meant he was in his late thirties or early forties. Plump, balding, gentle; a gentle, thoughtful Swiss émigré, as though Switzerland were a country to be run from like Czechoslovakia or the DDR. I was taken by his earnestness, the way, in speaking, he seemed to confide. In the weeks we knew each other I managed to learn almost nothing about him. Was he poor? Hard to believe in the poor of Switzerland, in Swiss poverty. Was he the softly spoken ex-Minister of Culture flung out of office for making passes at teenage boys? Our conversations were abstract, slightly political, often focused on the rather crude power structures of Q Service: the Dutch overseers – *chefs* – and the entirely disposable boiler-suited polyglot labour force. But whatever else he was, however he had found his way to Q Service, I understood that he was a citizen of a place I was only passing through. To be cleaning the airport at nineteen was one thing, to be doing it at his age – an educated man, clearly so – spoke of a choice, a circumstance more interesting and more troubling than my own. He may simply have been a failure, pathetic. Or he may have been like Lenin in Zurich, biding his time and hunkered out of view until history caught up with him and he was launched.

We had trolleys loaded with mops, metal bins of boiling water and a range of cleaning agents of the kind you'd be wise not to spill on your bare hand. My beat was the engine hangar where jet engines hung in cradles of chain, each with its court of attendant technicians, crop-haired young men leaning into hatches, reaching in with their spanners and drills. Every time they loosened a bolt a stream of oil thick as molasses bled onto the concrete floor. My job was to clean it up, moving from slick to slick under the shadows of the engines (sublime objects in their way, all that dense functionality). Ten-hour shifts, the hours punctuated by visits to a vending machine for coffee and chocolate. Then the Spacevan back to the city, a glass of beer at the bar beside the drop-off, and we were done – the Swiss returning to his room or rooms (room, I think) in the suburbs, while I was at the Sleep-Inn again, paying my six guilders and lying down on the foam, my clothes, my skin, giving off the smell of the work, metallic, chemical. It was a job that might have served as a model of drudgery, yet I found something soothing in it. See oil, clean it up, fetch more hot water, repeat. I wondered if I might be especially suited to it. A number of my recent schoolmasters, fond of telling me how the scrapheap awaited, might have said so. And if you gave up on conventional ideas of success – success as money, as power – could you not live perfectly well performing the simplest tasks while keeping something of yourself, the something that mattered, entirely free? I thought of T.E. Lawrence rejoining the army as a private soldier in the years between the wars and saying how relaxing it was, taking orders from fools. Then I gave it up with barely a shrug in exchange for a job in a bakery that involved no minibus ride, paid slightly more and would, I hoped, be easier. I handed in my overalls, said goodbye to my Swiss, my fellow oily. I shook his hand. I don't think either of us had the least expectation of ever seeing each other again. (Such is the mode of knowing the drifting life implies. Each thing for a while then not. Each man or woman, then not.)

For a few days I was free and exchanged my mask of proletarian hero for that of flâneur, took long rambles around the city, head full of leafy summer air, book in pocket (the stories of Heinrich von Kleist), now and then pausing on a bench to roll a little spliff, watch girls, watch water, watch and be watched by the tourists in the low, glass-roofed boats. In cramped handwriting I wrote things, observations, lines of poetry, little truths I probably lost within days of writing them. I think I was very happy.

The bakery was not as quaint as it had sounded – a modest industrial unit, a small factory, twenty minutes' walk from the Sleep-Inn. It only had one product, a type of toasted bread they sliced into guilder-sized roundels and bagged up like crisps or crackers. The loaves, as dough, were laid in narrow moulds in metal trays, each tray perhaps a metre long. The trays came down the line to where I stood in a new set of overalls ready to load them into the oven. If the trays collided, the dough shortened, losing a quarter-inch from either end. The boss fretted over this, instructing us to treat the loaves like children – *kinderen* – but the moment he was gone (he was always hurrying from one room to another) I took great delight in car-crashing the trays and watching the loaves jump in their skins

– terrified worms, sinister white *kinderen*. This kind of petty sabotage must be common in all factories where the worker knows he has no real human value in the place he spends the greater part of his day. A protest against the work that is, in part, a protest against work itself. As for the bosses, their irascibility is all bad conscience. They understand the insult perfectly. It spoils their lunches, puts grey shadows under the eyes of their listless daughters . . .

When I grew bored of tormenting the dough babies I signed on for a new job out of the city, a canning factory in the south not far from Breda where, in the Velázquez painting, the Dutch General surrenders to the Spanish General in a scene of high chivalry, the two men gesturing like dancers, seemingly embarrassed to meet in such circumstances, anxious to distance themselves from the reality of violence. A more recent war felt close enough in the Netherlands. In Amsterdam I had visited the Anne Frank House and for several hours had been unable to move past what I found there. And in the small town we now arrived outside, the retreating German army, in one of those acts of casual savagery they were so willing to perform, blew up the *stadhuis* along with a large part of the town's inhabitants who were sheltering in the cellars. In 1979, across much of Europe, the war was still ending, a background radiation of trauma and grief and exhaustion that had not yet expended itself. When you said 'the war', nobody wondered which one you were talking about.

We lived in a camp in the countryside, a mile or two out of town, in a marquee that would have covered most of a soccer pitch, already well used by the time I got there. With old pallets people had blocked off spaces that gave no privacy but which created room-sized zones, slightly preferable to bedding down in a bare, open space like the survivors of a disaster. In my 'room' there were, perhaps, a dozen of us – English, Irish, French, Portuguese. The place was filthy but not oppressive. Light seeped through the canvas walls. The Duma smoke, the dope smoke, blew through the open flaps. Rats, I think, were afraid to come in.

There was a night shift but I didn't work it. My turn came in the early mornings when we gave up our space and sometimes our sleeping bags to those returning from the factory. Though it was high summer those daybreaks always had a chill to them, a coolness of water that spread from the fat curves of the nearby river. There was a blockhouse for people who liked to wash. For the rest, a half-hour to stand about smoking, watching the trees shrug off their night shadows.

My job was to pack gherkins into large clear jars or, more precisely – for each part of the process was broken down into the smallest possible units of work – I pushed the gherkins down into the clear liquid the jars contained (some sort of highly spiced brine), submerged them by slapping the glass collar of a passing jar with the flat of my palm or thumping it with the base of a fist.

Along with the foreign workers from the big tent there were girls and women who were bussed in from somewhere else, across the border in Belgium perhaps, or from a Flemish-speaking community in the south. Feisty, good-natured, their hair in nets, their feet in rubber boots, they were long-accustomed to the work, left it to their hands and laughed at us as we tried to keep pace with the machinery. At least once each shift there were gherkin fights. The women always started it. They knew what would be tolerated, were on home ground or nearly so, and did not have the appearance of people who would be easily intimidated by the men in white coats, the overseers, the *chefs*. They threw and we threw back, lobbed gherkins across the lines as fast as we could grab them, two minutes of anarchy, of boys and girls, the irrepressible, the air briefly darkening, greening . . .

As in all such work, especially the last hour or two of a shift, weary from standing, nothing for the mind to latch on to, people grew careless. One afternoon the boy next to me, his job to catch the jars I missed, brought down his fist on the glass, brought it down too hard, shattered the glass and drove a shard through the rubber of his glove and deep into his hand. A swirl of red in the brine, a twisting cloud of it. We led him out. The belt rattled onwards, carrying now its special bloody edition of a savoury favourite. The women, seeing what had happened but sticking to their tasks, called out to us in kind voices, words we did not understand.

And like soldiers we were redeployed to other fronts as the need arose. When things slackened with the gherkins there was a call from the peas and beans facility. A harvest was coming in; lorries from the fields were queuing at the gates. I moved from the big tent into the town, a hostel for *gastarbeiders*, Kurdish men mostly. There were no women. It was an old house, quite substantial and properly fitted out for its purpose with showers and fire doors and a small mosque. Outside was a bicycle shelter. Next door was a bar.

The new work involved another mechanical belt but this time I was in a large, open-sided shelter, had a seat rather than having to stand, and did not have to risk puncturing myself with broken glass. Next to me sat one of the Kurds from the hostel, a small man with a gorgeous moustache that he must, in his mornings at the hostel, have tended like a piece of beloved topiary. Our mission was to pick from the belt little frogs and the occasional rodent that had been hoovered up by the field machinery and now passed in front of us like shipwrecked mariners on a sea of beans. We seized them and put them into jars, and for each one caught there was a small premium, a three-guilder reward for sparing the customer the shock of opening a bag of veg and finding a pair of eyes staring up at her. We displayed our catches to each other in a spirit of friendly competition, exchanged grins and nods suggestive of congratulation, of admiration for the skills involved – quickness of eye, quickness of hand – all of it, each glance and shrug and twitch of the moustache veined with irony, as if we were princes in disguise, exiled lords who, through some freakish tide of history, were temporarily employed hunting the tiny and the inoffensive.

I settled down, or I breathed out, or I simply arrived, as if the time before had been a kind of falling and now, rather than air, I had earth under my boots. When I wasn't working I strolled to the edge of town and watched summer burning like a slow fuse. Or I hung out in the bar beside the hostel, with its booths and dark wood, its jukebox and faded photograph of Queen Juliana.

There was a barmaid called Lilli. She was from Yugoslavia, a Serb, though we were, most of us, still ten years away from our education in the various ethnic groupings of that place. Whenever the bar was quiet I found some excuse to speak to her. From the beginning, despite the small difference in our ages (twenty-six to nineteen) she treated me as experience treats innocence, seemed merely amused at such attentions, the brass of it. But I knew enough, or guessed enough, to understand that what she saw – a young man with the unfakeably clear eye of the newly hatched – touched her, and that beneath her self-possession, her barmaid's look-but-don't-touch, there was a sentimental appetite that would nag at her like the beginning of a minor illness. We started meeting up, taking walks beside the river, or Dutch-style bunk-up bike rides along flat roads between painterly trees. I was invited – a mark of high confidence – to attend the Saturday night/Sunday morning/Sunday afternoon salons at her house, where a mongrel collection of locals and passers-through gathered with their drugs of choice. My own drug of choice – good grass – I bought at one of the banks in town, or from someone who lived in the bank and who, once the bank had shut, would respond to a knock on the door and sell one or two of those little pungent bags, whatever my mouse money, my frog money, could pay for. I think now I was less surprised by this than I should have been – a drug dealer in a bank – but I was no longer the new boy and had begun to be familiar with the music of away, the potential for doors to lead anywhere, the likelihood of it.

The night we became lovers her boyfriend showed up. She had, I suppose, forgotten to tell him about the new circumstance. I sat on the end of the bed while they argued in Dutch. Neither of them looked at me. The man raised his voice; Lilli stood her ground. Had he shoved her or struck her I like to imagine I would have done something more than just sit on the bed, adrenaline making my hands shake. He left at last, down the stairs still shouting, then out the front door, a final complaint flung like gravel at the window. Somehow the night was repaired. Assurances and comforting led to kisses, a slow crawl up the bed, the comedy and tenderness of undressing someone who, a fortnight earlier, I did not know existed.

'Not bad for a boy,' she said, when we finished. We rolled cigarettes by touch, that lovely, sweet Dutch tobacco, lay shoulder to shoulder in the dark. It was late August and the nights were almost cold. By then, I had already started wondering how long I would stay, had taken deep glances into possible futures, at least one of them with Lilli. Stay away until away became home. Why not? People did it. And what was waiting for me in England? Nothing obvious, nothing I could easily name, only that its character would be different – weightier, less free. But even as I had such thoughts I knew they were just a private dreaming, and that my season of away, unlike the Swiss in Amsterdam, the Kurds in the hostel, unlike Lilli, was almost done. I fretted about telling her and when, in late September, I did, she cried, though only briefly. It was, of course, exactly as she had expected.

On my last day in the town I went to see her. She had wrapped up a dozen fragments of hash, none bigger than a rosary bead, and between kisses and teasing and the recovery of her barmaid's bravado, she pushed them deep into the pockets of my coat, my trousers, so that I was still finding them at the ferry port where I tried to hide them more carefully. The ferry was a night-sailing. I sat out on deck to watch the lights of the Hook grow small. At some point a girl my own age, blonde, tipsy, a total stranger, sat beside me, told me her troubles, then fell asleep against my shoulder. She was still there, wrapped in her coat and sleeping like a child, when the sun rose and I saw the first of England. In every sea-facing window a fire. ∎

'The borders weren't falling, they were going up again . . . And then a man was back in the cage he'd been born into, the cage called Fatherland, which dangled along with a bunch of other cages called Fatherland, all on a rod, which a great collector of cages and peoples was carrying deeper into history . . . But he didn't want to sit in a cage, access to which was controlled by the police, who only let you out with a passport that you had to get off the head of the cage, and then it went on from there, you stood in the inhospitable space between cages, and you rubbed up against all the bars, and to get into one of the other cages you needed something called a visa, a residence permit from the head of that cage. He didn't like giving permission.'
– Wolfgang Koeppen, *The Hothouse*, first published 1953, translated from the German by Michael Hofmann

The image of a row of birdcages carried on a pole over a man's shoulder comes from a novel of the early Cold War period. It is expressive of the idea of an alliance, of jealousy and unwieldiness. For all its flimsiness, the cage takes itself terribly seriously, restricting access, glorying in the name of Fatherland. The birds are kept segregated or isolated. It is all too easy to imagine the plight of a bird that has got out, or that is visiting – bird markets are always attended by free spirits like pigeons and starlings and sparrows, fascinated by a kinship of species, and maybe too by the presence of seed and feed – and now finds herself being rubbed to pieces between prisons. I wanted to share Koeppen's rather Brueghel-ish image. For Europe, and indeed the world, it is a bleak moment, when internal and external communication is once again impeded, when the skip into an adjacent cage requires papers, and when the individual bird is forced to swim for her life. ■

THE POETICS OF TRAUMA

Ulf Karl Olov Nilsson

TRANSLATED FROM THE SWEDISH BY PETER GRAVES

I spent twenty-five years in psychiatry, the last eleven as a psychologist. In the 1990s I worked for five years in the acute ward at Lillhagen Hospital in Gothenburg and had many sessions with people under threat of deportation; these were cases in which linguistic analysis – as it is called – had been the decisive factor in the official refusal of permission to remain in Sweden. Linguistic analysis is the controversial and much criticised method used by the Swedish Migration Agency in its attempts to determine whether a refugee actually comes from the country she or he claims to have come from.

For several months during this time I was talking to a girl of African origin in her late teens. The staff of the ward knew little more about her than that her application for asylum had been rejected, and that she was about to be deported. She had undergone linguistic analysis in French, her second language, and been informed that the conclusion was that she did not come from the country she claimed. How this linguistic analysis was carried out was something of a mystery since her primary symptoms were that she did not speak at all, and did nothing but stare at the wall while lying semi-recumbent in a hospital bed. Or perhaps she had spoken to some extent before the analysis, and become mute afterwards. Maybe she had felt under suspicion and experienced the linguistic analysis as an interrogation or accusation: 'Anything you say may be used against you.'

All that remained for her was humanity's last legal resort – the right to remain silent. Doctors and psychiatric nurses had been trying without success for a week or so to get her to say something. Now it was my turn. I led her into a consulting room, sat her in a chair and began asking questions, sometimes in Swedish, sometimes in French: *Do you know where you are? What's your name? Do you have any family? Would you like a glass of water? Did you sleep last night? My goodness, look at that rain! And now the sun's shining! If you understand what I'm saying, just nod.*

Since she didn't answer, indeed made no response at all, I started to do the talking myself, telling her things such as that I knew her application for asylum had been rejected; that she was in a psychiatric clinic; that it was now summer in Sweden. She didn't even look at me, just rocked catatonically back and forth in her chair. Our second conversation began in the same way, but at one point I asked her: *Est-ce que tu penses que tu es folle? Do you think that you are mad?* At last she looked up and gave some sign of contact. I repeated the question, which she clearly found painful; it had probably finally sunk in that she was in a psychiatric hospital, and presenting the condition psychiatrists call 'stupor'.

She started crying then and was finally able, haltingly and in fragments, at length, but also *very carefully*, to tell a story that was as unspeakably sad and brutal as it is possible to imagine. When she was fourteen years old her parents had been shot in front of her; her brothers had tried to run away but had probably been killed, and she herself had been locked in a cellar where for a month she had been repeatedly raped by her jailers until she eventually managed to escape through a ventilation hole.

Did I have any reason to doubt this young woman? It was quite obvious that the Swedish Migration Agency had disbelieved her. According to the linguistic analysis, she came from a neighbouring, more peaceful country than the one she had named.

There are a number of fundamental questions we need to ask ourselves when we meet and work with vulnerable people. What are the criteria of truth in a conversation? Are all statements either true or false? If a refugee who has been persecuted and tortured finds herself in a situation that feels like an interrogation, is her ability to express herself affected? What are the linguistic effects of trauma? Why is silence, or enigmatic obscurity, so often the linguistic expression of trauma? To what extent is silence a performance, a protest perhaps, and when is silence a symptom?

One of the basic concepts of psychoanalysis is that the neurotic symptom is a compromise between an impulse and the defence against the impulse. The impulse can only express itself by disguise, by paraphrase. In other words, the symptom may be viewed as a metaphor. In his 1917 series of lectures Freud used the following allegory:

> Let us therefore compare the system of the unconscious to a large entrance hall, in which the mental impulses jostle one another like separate individuals. Adjoining this entrance hall there is a second, narrower, room – a kind of drawing room – in which consciousness, too, resides. But on the threshold between these two rooms a watchman performs his function: he examines the different mental impulses, acts as a censor, and will not admit them into the drawing room if they displease him . . .

Thus the neurotic symptom is a way of trying to articulate the forbidden *in a different way*, as a kind of condensed compromise produced in the struggle between internal irreconcilable wills.

If the neurotic symptom is a coded message which, nevertheless, it is sometimes possible to understand and interpret, the main symptoms of the trauma sufferer – recurring flashbacks and nightmares – are of a different, more literal, quality. They are transparent: victims of violence dream of the violence they have suffered, or possibly of certain details surrounding that violence. The symptoms of the trauma sufferer derive from history, not from the unconscious. But trauma is also characterised by a silence, a secretiveness, an unwillingness to tell the story.

How are we to understand the difficulties, and reluctance, faced by victims of trauma when they are asked to tell their stories? Cathy Caruth, in her important anthology *Trauma: Explorations in Memory*, writes that truth for the victim of trauma does not reside in simple brutal facts but rather in the way that the traumatising event defies comprehension: 'The flashback or traumatic re-enactment conveys, that is, both *the truth of an event,* and *the truth of its incomprehensibility.'*

Thus trauma is not a catalogued memory, an archived event, but a contradictory force which has no proper location within the psyche. Classifying it is beyond both human experience and the possibilities of language. Trauma lies beyond simple memory, which is why it returns as involuntary thoughts and flashbacks.

A fundamental difficulty when dealing with survivors of trauma is finding the strength to linger on the silent, enigmatic literalness of the traumatic event without eliminating the force and truth of the experience. As Emily Dickinson expresses it:

If any ask me why –
'Twere easier to die –
Than tell –

Psychologists and therapists, not to mention artists, journalists and employees of the Migration Agency who want to study the effects of trauma, should at least have some understanding of how to avoid undermining trauma testimony with well-intended language. They must be aware of how their engagement can become a burden, one more horrific experience among the many already suffered.

Victims of trauma are faced with a dilemma: they may experience opening up and speaking about the trauma as a surrender of the most tangible reality in their lives. This, the refusal to let go and give up the

object, is at the heart of trauma, its great and perhaps only defence –
one that it shares with melancholia. This was one of the things that was
at stake when the health workers were trying to help the African girl.

'The staff say that you just sit in your room all day every day.'

'Yes.'

'What do you do there?'

'Nothing.'

'Do you daydream about things?'

'No.'

'Do you think about anything?'

'No.'

'Are you sad? Do you cry sometimes? Do you think about your
parents?'

'No.'

'Do you sleep? Do you walk around? Do you just sit and look?'

'I look.'

'What do you look at?'

'Nothing.'

And that, we might add, is precisely what she had tried to do when
she was locked in the cellar. In *Beyond the Pleasure Principle* Freud
writes: 'But I am not aware that the patients suffering from traumatic
neuroses are much occupied in waking life with the recollection of
what happened to them. They perhaps strive rather not to think of it.'

The view of the Swedish Immigration Agency is that some
people who apply for refugee status do not tell the truth about
where they come from. There are normally about 2,000 calls for
linguistic analysis per year in Sweden. The basis of such an analysis is
a recording lasting some fifteen minutes in which the asylum seeker is
interviewed, usually by telephone, about his or her origin and way of
life. Then it is up to a linguistic analyst from the country in question
– or at least from the region – to decide whether the applicant is
from the specified area, or not. Where possible, the language analysed
is the asylum seeker's mother tongue, but often the interview must

take place in their second language, which is almost always French or English.

Linguistic analysis, which has been in use in Sweden since 1993, has been widely scrutinised. In 2014 the Swedish Migration Board, as it was called then, was severely criticised by the UK Supreme Court, for instance, which pointed both to the defective analytic methodology and to clearly substandard reporting. An international network of legal linguists, the International Association of Forensic Linguists, has warned the authorities not to determine asylum seekers' nationality on the basis of speech alone.

L et us think for a moment about the relationship between language and geography. Consider, for instance, such basic issues as class, education, dialect, or even just the importance of family background when it comes to pronunciation and vocabulary. Remember that refugees often come from parts of the world where many different languages are spoken, or where one and the same language is spoken in a number of countries. It becomes quite obvious that linguistic analysis should only be approached with the utmost care and caution, if at all.

To this, we should also add a criticism from the psychological perspective: trauma involves a crisis in relation to language and to truth. The fact that what occurred is experienced as *too much* makes it difficult to remember and to understand what really happened: the victim of trauma has reason to mistrust language itself as well as his or her interlocutors, since there is a risk that the subject will be abused or her experience disparaged. Thus, the essence of real trauma lies in its incomprehensibility – if it can be understood, then it arguably isn't trauma. A reading of linguistic analysis reports makes it quite clear that hesitant speech, latency in response, memory problems – precisely the things that characterise the speech of those who suffer from trauma or depression – are regularly interpreted as dissimulation and lies.

What are the chances, then, for the traumatic event to be given a linguistic, artistic and potentially therapeutic and healing form?

I would argue that a fundamental problem of trauma is that it runs the risk of presenting itself, or being forced to present itself, as a cliché, as self-exploitation, or, worse still, as a combination of both – a sentimental playing to the gallery. I agree with literary critic Shoshana Felman when she writes that in the same way that literature is often trivialised by literary interpretation, trauma is often trivialised by psychoanalytic attempts to psychologise.

Claude Lanzmann, the director of the Holocaust documentary *Shoah*, talked about the obscenity of the question, 'Why have the Jews been killed?' Whichever explanation historians and psychologists may choose (unemployment in Germany, Hitler's childhood, his disciplinarian father, the historic persecution of Jews), the question itself, according to Lanzmann, is both limiting and indecent. The refusal to understand is, for him, an ethical imperative. In the case of the girl threatened with deportation, I would argue that the obscenity takes something like the following form: 'We believe that you are telling the truth. We believe you when you say that you saw your parents killed when you were fourteen years old and that you were raped hundreds of times – so now you will be allowed to stay in Sweden.'

The fear that their traumatic experiences will be denigrated and belittled is perhaps most obvious among Holocaust survivors, who sometimes voice the feeling that they belong to a special group of *Geheimnisträger* – bearers of secrets. But it is a common fear found in all clinical settings dealing with trauma, and presumably also in their literary equivalents. I think of trauma as waging a sort of war to avoid banal interpretations. Let me propose six tools used in this struggle:

1) *Condensation*: to express oneself in terms difficult to understand, cryptically even, and never – or only very discreetly – mention the trauma in concrete terms.

2) *Displacement*: to talk or write about details secondary to what was truly traumatising, making them, implicitly or otherwise, carry the symbolic load of the trauma.

3) *Simplification*: to approach and name the event as simply, clearly, honestly and in as neutral a way as possible, in a manner that may seem emotionally disconnected.

4) *Ignorance*: to disregard knowledge and deny all understanding and explanation of the trauma. To approach the traumatic event with a consciously naive and unknowing gaze in order to allow a retelling of the story.

5) *Excess*: to express oneself too much, to talk at length, be long-winded, boring or overly detailed, thus excluding the possibility of dialogue. The subtext is, you are asking me for *the most important part*, but I can only give you *everything*.

6) *Implacability*: to refuse cooperation, community, comprehension or readability. Or, quite simply, to refuse to speak.

The work of the American Jewish objectivist poet Charles Reznikoff (1894–1976) tells us something about the potential of literature on trauma. In his long and unfinished work *Testimony: The United States of America, 1885–1915: Recitative*, he strove for forty years to pare down, simultaneously condensing and simplifying, American law reports from the late nineteenth and early twentieth centuries. His aim was a new kind of poem in which the course of events, and nothing but the course of events, would be present in its purest form. In an interview Reznikoff said the following:

> Well, I take the original source and edit it and edit it. In many cases I keep the language. I sometimes change it, but rarely. I do change the language if it doesn't coincide with something that I think is simple and direct. But as a rule, I just edit, that is, I throw out everything.

He cuts expressions of emotion, value judgements, Latinisms, difficult terms and second-hand information such as legal discussions and judgements. What remains is the event itself, transferred from a judicial to a poetic context. The French poet Emmanuel Hocquard calls Reznikoff's work translations 'from American into American'. Hocquard continues:

> What makes this work so revolutionary is precisely its literalness, which is the opposite to literature. The doubling reveals the model in a new light, logically, mercilessly, unbearably . . . They are the same words, the same phrases, but they are not the same statements. It is remarkable to observe that this small displacement of the same thing, this simple transition from one form to another in the same powerful way produces meaning and purifies it.

But is Reznikoff's work with *Testimony* really a translation? Yes, at least in the sense that, following a method that has been carefully thought through, he *transfers* a text from one context to another. If we consider the etymology of the word translation (from the Latin *translatus*, 'carried across') and allow ourselves a generous definition of the word, we get closer to a fundamental aspect of the very essence of writing poetry: the discovery and handling of poetic specificity. Suddenly it is no longer necessary to invent poetry, instead it's a matter of locating it, or giving it room to think. The poet's task is not to produce poetic content, but rather to recognise and transfer the subject matter to new contexts.

At the age of eighty or more Charles Reznikoff set about a new task: to use the same poetic method to compress some twenty volumes of reports from the Nuremberg trial and the Eichmann trial down to the one hundred pages of his long poem *Holocaust* (1975). It is notable that Reznikoff waited until that great age before starting work on the camps. In earlier interviews, when asked whether he was going to write about Auschwitz, he answered that the despair he felt about the camps was transferred to *Testimony*. But it is clear, nevertheless, that he could not let go of the Holocaust. His doubt came from his lack of first-hand experience: he had not 'been there', and he was uncertain whether his work was ethically or poetically justified.

Holocaust is divided into sections with headings such as 'Deportation', 'Invasion', 'Ghettos', 'Massacres', 'Children', 'Mass Graves' and, finally, 'Escapes'. We can sense a vague chronological order that points to a kind of exit from a darkness that would, perhaps, otherwise become overwhelmingly large. The following is taken from the section headed 'Children':

1

Once, among the transports, was one with children – two freight cars
    full.
The young men sorting out the belongings of those taken to the gas
    chambers
had to undress the children – they were orphans –
and then take them to the 'lazarette'.
There the SS men shot them.

2

A large eight-wheeled car arrived at the hospital
where there were children:
in the two trailers – open trucks – were sick women and men
lying on the floor.
The Germans threw the children into the trucks
from the second floor and the balconies –
children from one year old to ten:
threw them upon the sick in the trucks.
Some of the children tried to hold on to the walls,
scratched at the walls with their nails:
but the shouting Germans
beat and pushed the children towards the windows.

3

...

A visitor once stopped one of the children:
a boy of seven or eight, handsome, alert and gay.
He had only one shoe and the other foot was bare,
and his coat of good quality had no buttons.
The visitor asked him his name
and then what his parents were doing:
and he said, 'Father is working in the office
and Mother is playing the piano.'
Then he asked the visitor if he would be joining his parents soon –
they always told the children they would be leaving soon to rejoin
    their parents –
and the visitor answered, 'Certainly. In a day or two.'
At that the child took out of his pocket
half an army biscuit he had been given in camp
and said, 'I am keeping this half for Mother';
and then the child who had been so gay
burst into tears.

Reznikoff believed that his juridical approach provided the very basis for his poetry. In his 1977 essay, 'First, there is the Need', he wrote:

> With respect to the treatment of subject matter in verse
> and the use of the term 'objectivist' and 'objectivism,' let
> me again refer to the rules with respect to testimony in a
> court of law. Evidence to be admissible in a trial cannot
> state conclusions of fact: it must state the fact themselves.

His use of testimony should not, however, be thought of as blind faith in the importance of the court or the law; *Holocaust* should not be understood as a trial in which the guilty are called to account. Reznikoff wants, rather, to make use of the rhetoric of the court to access what actually happened – and he insists that this rhetoric shares the seriousness of the questions it deals with. We cannot, however, claim that Reznikoff is trying to achieve a form of neutral documentation or reconciliation: the inherent brutality of the crimes and his selection of testimony exclude that. In his work, Reznikoff is acting not as a witness, but possibly as *a witness of the witnesses*, or perhaps even more as an editor of the witnesses.

When I translated Reznikoff's poem *Holocaust* into Swedish I absorbed his apprehensions. I had a strange and at times extremely unpleasant sensation of working with something my experience could not accommodate, something I quite simply had nothing to do with. If it is true that an important motive for the desire to translate a text is to investigate it – not just to understand it, but also to see what it can do – then, obviously, the issue is particularly pointed when the subject is the Holocaust. I could only translate slowly and in manageable segments, meanwhile immersing myself in essential Holocaust literature: Primo Levi, Hannah Arendt, Imre Kertész, Shoshana Felman. While working on the translation I thought that the method of writing, the disposition, that Reznikoff had come up with offered both a necessary and sober distance and an approach beyond an explanatory, psychologising interpretation of the Holocaust. Auschwitz, the great catastrophe of modernity, has, of course, been intensely scrutinised in films, TV series, literature and art. Reznikoff's cycle of poems may make us angry, shocked and full of despair, but the account given by the survivors is a confirmation, not a surprise. Reznikoff's purpose is not to discover, reveal and present us with something new, but to make us look *with new eyes* and, significantly, he does so by reduction rather than addition. He is not the narrator – there is no narrative voice. What is left instead, after all the revisions and revisions of revisions, is the voice of the witness and the precise details which resist efforts to read allegorically or metaphorically. It is the mass of distilled facts that gives the narrative a chance to speak for itself, allowing as much as possible to remain unsaid. Thus,

Reznikoff's Auschwitz does not become a metaphysical symbol for evil in the world, but a real place where men and women lived and died, worked and were murdered.

With *Holocaust* Reznikoff achieves something that I would like to call an umbilical moment, the moment when opposites meet, the point of the body where outside becomes inside and inside becomes outside. Reznikoff's poetry, extremely conceptual and ideas-based, becomes existential, but the opposite is also true: his fundamentally existential work also manifests itself precisely by becoming conceptual. This point can be illustrated with a pun that plays on the ambiguity of the word *subject* in English (which will, of course, also work with the French *sujet*). The word *subject* in English corresponds to *I*, to the nominative case, but it can also mean *topic*. In existential poetry it is the ego that is the subject, the topic: the poet is writing about him or herself and his or her life. In conceptual poetry the situation is the opposite in that it is the topic of the poetry that speaks, that is its ego. In existential poetry, then, *the subject is the subject* (the ego is its topic), while in conceptual poetry the situation is the exact reverse, namely *the subject is the subject* (the topic is its ego) – amazingly, the same thing!

Some years after our last conversation, the African girl rang me quite out of the blue. She said she was pregnant and was about to get married. She told me – without me asking – that the man was kind and that she herself was working as a home carer. When I asked whether she wanted to come and talk, she said no: 'There's no need. I just wanted to tell you.'
    'OK, all the best.'
    'Thank you.'
    'Take care of yourself.'
    'I will.'
    'Bye, then.'
    'Bye.' ∎

Colin Herd

Fanciphobia

hello all of you
brilliant poets and poetry fans
such appetites etc
I was thinking
tomorrow morning
how about you
walk out of your jobs
and those without jobs walk into them just up and toodle-ooo
just up and hello nice to meet you
take the staple gun
fantasise interiors
my name all of a sudden is
if you could redecorate
one thing
my name all of a sudden is
I want to quit my job
and start negotiating
(I like my job)
take the coffee machine
that's going nowhere
trellised rose wallpaper
take the water cooler
I'm so anti-it I can't put

it into words there's a kind of exit
that never really happens
that is just ongoing –
like saying all the time the whole party
I need to go soon I need to go soon and
people keep offering you stuff and telling you stories
negotiate till doomsday
negotiate till kingdom come indulgence is desperate
I'm such a flatterer
You are all so brilliant
You've written good poems
many of you have
I want to print out all your poems and scrunch them up
and stuff them in my clothes maybe read them first!
just maybe / no promises
my favourite Romantic poet is
Anna Laetitia Barbauld
I wear my fear around me
I fan it out on my pillow
and spray my pillow with it
I've never been moved by staff meetings
I hated *Call Me By Your Name*
except the conversation with a fish

and the clothes
the conversations with people
all through were so horrible
and then I watched it with someone who
hated it and I started to like it more
but *God's Own Country* I didn't have so much beef with
except the crouchy
wash was borrowed wholesale
from *Brokeback Mountain*
my name all of a sudden is Mark Kermode
good evening to you all
it's the audience that makes a performance
you are sleeping with stuff attached to you
you are car-less and sometimes annoying
but I don't hold that against you

BINIDITTU

Nicola Lo Calzo

Introduction by Daisy Lafarge

It's perhaps a truism that acts of devotion both make and unmake the devotional object. Over centuries, pilgrims' gestures of love – stroking and kissing – infinitesimally erode statues and relics representative of the divine. In seeking transcendence the devotee reinforces the object's transience, a paradox that reveals attention as a physical force. Love is a tarnish; no object is left unmarked by the state of being adored. In Christian Europe the furies of iconoclasm left an indelible question mark over attempts to represent the divine. One further ambiguity might be likened to a devotional mirror stage: how important is it that in representations of the sacred we are able to glimpse something of ourselves?

Set in Sicily and spread across its streets, sacred spaces and sites of marginalised labour, Italian photographer Nicola Lo Calzo's *Binidittu* project grapples with these issues of recognition and representation. Portraits of mostly young black men – some from West Africa seeking asylum in Europe, others the children of an earlier generation of migrants – are set against the devotional context of Benedetto the Moor, a sixteenth-century Afro-Sicilian who became the first black saint. While some of Lo Calzo's images play directly with hagiography, framing these young men as saintly icons, others orbit Benedetto's diasporic legacy by way of mass-produced souvenirs, and traces of his veneration in Sicilian streets and buildings. *Binidittu* continues Lo Calzo's project of documenting the African diaspora around the world, and his draw to Sicily is understandable: the island and its capital Palermo have long functioned as the crossroads of Europe and Africa, pivotal in the flux of people and trade from slavery to present-day migration.

B orn to enslaved parents around 1526 and declared free at birth, Benedetto Manasseri was a priest and healer who bore the name of the Sicilian family that owned his father. He grew up to become a pastor and later joined a Franciscan convent where he preached, healed the sick and worked as a cook until his death in 1589. In the following centuries Benedetto became a hugely popular figure, not only in Sicily but also across Europe and South America, where his devotional cult was spread by Spanish and Portuguese colonialists. While Benedetto's blackness has been a cause for celebrity in Latin America, his native Sicily tells a different story. In the rising tensions around slavery in the eighteenth century, Benedetto's ethnicity was seen as too politically charged, resulting in the longest canonisation debate in history. His sainthood was eventually confirmed in 1807, the same year that slavery was abolished in Britain.

The whitewashing of Benedetto took a number of forms. His status as Sicily's patron saint was supplanted by the twelfth-century St Rosalia, and a pink-white Christ child was introduced to depictions of the black saint. While St Rosalia still dominates Sicily today, the Confraternity of Benedetto il Moro boasts 140 members devoted to the saint's processions, relics and feast days. At first it is immensely heartening to see Lo Calzo's images of white Sicilian men venerating the figure of a black man. But the interviews collected for the project indicate something more sinister; many of these men do not believe that Benedetto was ethnically 'black', and definitely not black like the many young migrant men in Sicily's towns.

This dissonant exceptionalism is nothing new in the history of the Church. In her lucid book on the myth and cult of the Virgin Mary, *Alone of All Her Sex*, Marina Warner writes of the fierce debate around the tradition of black Madonnas, and how explanations other than race have been sought to justify their existence. While many suggest that these figures were simply carved from ebony, rendering any ethnic resemblance coincidental, others suggest that the Madonnas 'blackened' over time by exposure to the smoke from votive candles. Yet neither of these theories can be easily disentangled from medieval Christianity's fraught relationship with race, where blackness was often viewed in allegorical terms drawn from passages in the Song of Songs. The famed twelfth-century 'love letters' of Abelard and Héloïse contain a lengthy passage from Abelard concerning the blackness of Moses' Ethiopian wife; for Abelard, the black woman's outer 'affliction' made her all the 'purer' within, and suggests this correlated to heightened sexual pleasure for her husband. Blackness, Abelard wrote, kept Moses' wife 'humble and abject in this life so that she may be exalted in the next'. Similarly, Warner iterates that despite Catholicism's association of blackness with the devil and the occult, 'Black Madonnas are considered especially wonder-working, as the possessors of hermetic knowledge and power.'

This twinning of reification and disavowal leads to a contradictory state of hyper-visible invisibility. 'I am overdetermined from the outside,' Frantz Fanon wrote, 'I am a slave not to the "idea" others have of me, but to my appearance.' The images of *Binidittu* brush up against such states of fragile recognition, but are careful not to linger too long. Instead Lo Calzo follows his young male subjects from urban streets to the countryside, where many of them work *al campo* harvesting olives. The lived conditions of seasonal labour are cramped and difficult; most camps lack shower facilities and men often sleep four to a one-man tent. While the UN and NGOs have denounced this kind of labour as 'modern slavery', the workers stay because what they can earn in a day is better than in the city, where work is scarce and wages are biased against them. The Sicily Lo Calzo depicts is rife with tension, struggle and dislocation, but not without hope. One photograph documents a giant mural of Benedetto that was supported by the Antirazzista, one of many local groups working to combat racism and promote integration. Unlike the Benedetto figurines manufactured in China then shipped back to Italy, in this mural no white Christ child has been thrust into Benedetto's hands in an attempt to dilute his blackness.

The portraits of *Binidittu* reflect the historical valency of Benedetto's blackness, and its contemporary recalibration in the context of migration and rising populist sentiment. Weighed against the Sicilians who disbelieve Benedetto's ethnicity are a growing number of organisations and individuals to whom Benedetto symbolises hope and possibility. Among them is Friar Dieudonné Benedetto, an Ivorian who came to Sicily by boat and encountered the story of Benedetto while living in a migrant centre. In an unreservedly dramatic composition, the friar clasps his hands together and gazes up, as if at the source of divine illumination. Dieudonné tells Lo Calzo that he took Benedetto's name because he felt the saint was his guide in life, and that his friar's tunic protects him from the invisibility suffered by his migrant brothers. For many Sicilians images of Benedetto may fade into the background of everyday life, but for the undocumented lives of those working *al campo*, the veneration of a black man born to slaves represents nothing short of a revolution. ■

Amadou, from Dakar, in Palermo since 2013

Street scene, Palermo

Oumar Kamara, asylum seeker, during a performance at the International Puppet Museum

Mural of St Benedetto the Moor, Palermo

Confraternity of the
Holy Mother of Sorrows
of the Venerated Saint

The chapel of the
Chiesa del Gesù,
Palermo

Abdul, from Côte d'Ivoire, at Mondello Beach, Palermo

Open the Ports demonstration, Palermo

Campobello di Mazara camp

The procession of St Rosalia, patron saint of Palermo

Benedetto with the Christ child in the gift shop, Convent of Santa Maria di Gesù, Palermo

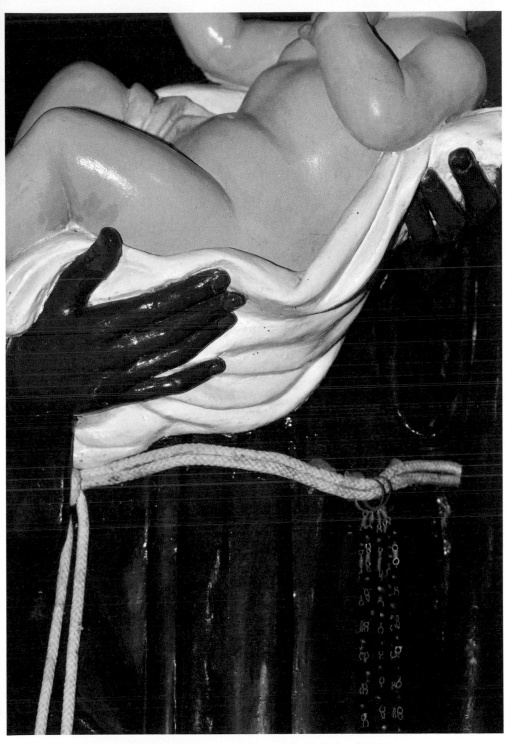

Statue of St Benedetto the Moor, Convent of Santa Maria di Gesù, Palermo

Friar Dieudonné Benedetto

A radical new take on the American family saga – the highly anticipated new novel from the acclaimed author of *Leaving the Atocha Station* and *10:04*.

'*The Topeka School* is a novel of exhilarating intellectual inquiry, penetrating social insight and deep psychological sensitivity . . . To the extent that we can speak of a future at present, I think the future of the novel is here'
SALLY ROONEY

'Ben Lerner's most essential and provocative creation yet'
CLAUDIA RANKINE

'Ben Lerner is a brilliant novelist, and one unafraid to make of the novel something truly new . . . He is one of my favourite living writers'
RACHEL KUSHNER

'*The Topeka School* is what happens when one of the most discerning, ambitious, innovative and timely writers of our day writes his most discerning, ambitious, innovative and timely novel to date'
MAGGIE NELSON

'*The Topeka School* is brave, furious and finally a work of love'
OCEAN VUONG

'Ben Lerner is a masterful writer who destabilises the very notion of what a novel can achieve by making it new at every turn. *The Topeka School* is not only a fiction for our times, but for the ages: insightful, humane, politically astute and true'
HILTON ALS

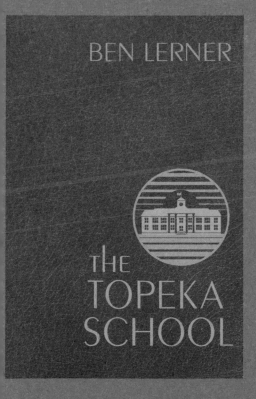

BEN LERNER

THE TOPEKA SCHOOL

Available November 2019

'Well then, eliminate the people, curtail them, force them to be silent. Because the European Enlightenment is more important than people.'
– Fyodor Dostoevsky, *Notebooks for The Brothers Karamazov*, translated from the Russian by Edward Wasiolek

This is a quotation from a notebook Dostoevsky kept while writing *The Brothers Karamazov*. The novel explores the origins of the love–hate relationship that people sometimes have with Europe when they – like me – come from countries located at its peripheries that never quite manage to be European. There are many intellectuals living on the fringes of Europe who yearn for European values like democracy, equality, secularism, modernity, freedom and women's rights, and who would like to see these implemented in their own countries. But most of their countrymen do not share these liberal intellectuals' enthusiasm for the same values. So in countries like mine, intellectuals in pursuit of a dream of Europe will sometimes try to force the adoption of European values 'from above', enlisting the help of armies, tsars, shahs and sultans, or working through the machinery of the state. At times the well-meaning, state-sanctioned imposition of these values is used to justify oppression and cruelty, which can cause the people of these nations around the edges of Europe to repudiate modernisation and Europeanisation altogether. In some cases the public may feel inclined to adopt modernisation and European values, but find that it is the state that resists the change – or vice versa. In Dostoevsky's novels the people generally scorn Western values urged upon them by the authorities, supported by bureaucrats and intellectuals, and explicitly reject attempts to coerce their acceptance. I used this quotation as an epigraph to my novel *Snow*, published in 2002, to prepare the reader for the perennial problems caused by the imposition of modernity. The novel was constructed around the story of female university students whom the

Turkish state, in its pursuit of 'secularism' (that most important and precious of European discoveries), would not allow to attend classes because of the traditional headscarves they wore. In the part of the world where I come from, Europe is not just an ideal and a beautiful dream, it is also a dream that is very difficult to fulfil in harmony with the people. ∎

Translated from the Turkish by Ekin Oklap

Abandoned house in Mytilene, island of Lesbos, Greece. Previously, offices of the University of the Aegean

SIX KILOMETRES

Adam Weymouth

'Believers in a traditional Hellenophobia–Turkophobia would have stared at the sight of the Mytilene Greeks spreading farewell meals for their departing neighbours, and later accompanying them to the quay, where Christians and Mohammedans, who for a lifetime had been plowing adjacently and even sharing occasional backgammon games at village cafes, embraced and parted with tears. Then, seated on their heaped up baggage, with their flocks around them – the women weeping, the children hugging their pets, the gray-bearded babas all dignity, as is their wont – the Mytilene Muslims set forth for unknown Turkey.'
– *National Geographic*, November 1922

White beach blue sea white village blue sky. One half of a Greek flag. A single orange life jacket, washed up on the tideline.

Sometimes, across the sea, Turkey's mountainous hinterland is hazy, especially in the days before a storm. The haze is sand blown in from Egypt, or so the baker says, and when the rains come the cars end up filthy and streaked. She says it never used to be like this. On other days the land is vivid, the houses of the towns along the coastline as distinct and bleached as the stones beneath the silent water. A single fishing boat, far out, a single man bowed to his net.

The Greek-made map of Lesbos, tacked up on the wall of our apartment, gives this history of the island, the text set in the blank space of the island's largest gulf:

> In 1355 Lesbos was presented as a dowry to the Genoese prince Francesco I Gattilusio and in the ensuing years acquired considerable economic and military power. This heyday lasted until 1462, when Sultan Mohamed II captured the island from the Genoese masters. Lesbos was plunged into centuries of darkness under Ottoman domination, until it was liberated by the Greek navy in 1912.

At the narrowest point of the strait, Turkey is six kilometres away. The Greek mainland is more than one hundred. Every Thursday morning and every Saturday morning, Greeks haul empty suitcases onto the ferries that make the crossing from Mytilene to Ayvalık, and in the evenings they return, their bags stuffed with cheap electronics and cotton sheets. The shopkeepers cross too, and the Roma, who pick up terracotta pots to sell from out the backs of their cars. The Turkish lira is weak these days. The crossing is forty-five minutes, or an hour and a half on the cheap boat. Coming back at dusk, the fading peaks of Lesbos echo those of the Turkish mainland, set adrift from its mirror twin. On the island of Cunda, as the boat quits Ayvalık's harbour for the sea, the tower of the abandoned church of Taxiarchis, now a museum, still catches the late sun. As we dock the swifts are screaming, dipping to the water in the last of the light.

It is spring; it has come again. The swifts arrived last week. The direct flights start from Gatwick, packed with birdwatchers seeking the annual passage of the hawk and tern and stork. The migrant boats begin to cross, and they are given little choice as to whether they do so on a calm day or in a storm. Frontex and the Turkish coastguard step up their nighttime patrols of coastal waters. Volunteers arrive from the wealthier European countries for their weeks of work with one of the more than 150 NGOs that now populate the island. And one day, the butterflies appear.

I see them first on the airport road as I am walking out of the supermarket. They are making their way along the street, a little higher than the cars, a thin but constant stream of them. Orange flashes in the afternoon light. I am with my daughter, and she points up at them from her pushchair, and we stop and watch them for some minutes as they continue overhead, from south to north.

As we walk home they are everywhere, flooding the island like a wind. I find one smashed in the grille of a parked car and extract it. It is a painted lady; I know them from English gardens far from here. In the apartment, I look them up. The maps of their migrations have thick arrows like diagrams of war, commencing in the sub-Sahara and converging on Europe, crossing the Mediterranean where the waters are narrowest, some through Greece, others through Spain. None of them, apparently, take the Italian route. It is too far over open sea, and I suppose, in some sense, they have a choice.

Little is known about insect migrations. Animals and birds can be fitted with trackers that record their movements, but insects are too delicate. And it is not a single creature that makes the 8,047-kilometre journey from Chad or Niger or Benin to Europe and then back again each year. Instead it is the species that migrates, over a succession of generations. Each *Vanessa cardui*'s life lasts between ten and twenty-four days, and during that time the adult female must travel, mate and deposit eggs. The next stage of the journey will be continued by her offspring. They catch the high-altitude winds. It is one of the longest insect migrations in the world.

I go out on the balcony. I cannot see them any more. Just the crumpled, folded body of the one that I am holding in my hand.

Insect migrations also remain unknown because we do not notice them. The birdwatchers flying in from Gatwick with their spotting scopes are not here for the butterflies. Much of what is known about their passage through Europe comes from studies in 2009, when, according to one paper, the 'numbers of *V. cardui* migrating across Europe were so high that they raised awareness among the general public, with the result that a large number of people contributed to online surveys and made it possible to investigate with unprecedented detail the migration system in this part of the range'. Yet they remain mysterious. Only in 2014 did an expedition to the Sahel reveal where the painted ladies spend their winters. No one on Lesbos remembers them in numbers like this. They are, perhaps, alighting here and breeding, before their final push to northern Europe.

I am sitting on the veranda of a well-to-do cafe that could be in Vienna or Lisbon – high ceilings, petits fours, the waiters in black aprons and white shirts – and just over five and a half kilometres away is the largest refugee camp in Europe. Because my partner is working at the camp full-time I have been looking after our daughter. It is possible to be on Lesbos and have little idea the camp is here. There are signs, if you know to look for them. In the graffiti – NO BORDERS, FUCK FRONTIERS, BLUE STAMP FOR ALL. The occasional rough sleeper who has not yet registered or been picked up by the police. The struggling or shuttered restaurants in the fishing villages, finding business increasingly slow since Lesbos hit the news and the tourists deserted the island for other, less complicated holidays. Each morning I go down to the beach and swim out into a sea where thousands have drowned. Picking through the flotsam – a shoe, a lens from a pair of glasses, a cigarette lighter – and wondering whether these are objects lost carelessly overboard, or all that remains now of someone's tragedy. In the playground, the Greek parents that I speak to want to know about the camps. Are people still arriving? Are they still being transferred to the mainland? They were just about to have a clear-out, perhaps they could donate some clothes?

Beyond the cafe, fish shops line the cobbled street. The farmers are arriving in their pickups from the hills inland, the flatbeds stacked with crates of oranges and camomile and cherries, and setting up in the shade. It is early, and already it is clear that it will be hot, again.

Further down, in the former Turkish part of town, beyond the banks and the perfumers and the United Colours of Benetton, is Yeni Mosque. Pigeons clatter through the shade to alight on rusting girders that keep the crumbling arches spread. Suggestions of sacred texts in relief in the broken stonework. Cats lounging in squares of sunlight, and the courtyard full of mallow. And on the road towards the airport, following the coast: crumbling Ottoman mansions overlooking Turkey and the ocean, long since abandoned, now graffitied, squatted by anarchists, squatted by migrants, squatted by dogs. They are like something out of Márquez, their faded plasterwork and splintered shutters still shading rooms that were packed into trunks and shipped away a hundred years ago. The wisteria gone wild. Their gardens choked with waist-high grasses, the citrus trees unpicked, the orange fruit startlingly bright. Some of the Ottoman Muslims got rich here, a good living to be made trading olive oil and soap across this narrow stretch of water, when this stretch of water was just that, a trade route, and not one of the most dangerous stretches of water in the world.

I have invited Masoud Ghorbanpour to the cafe this morning for a coffee. Normally he would be in the camp's two-hour breakfast queue just now. Masoud crossed that water one year and seven months ago. He came here from Iran. He fled Tehran on the night of his daughter's birthday, and paid €11,250, cash, for safe passage to Germany. The smuggler was all assurances. Masoud never made it to Germany. A series of missteps, his money gone, he was shuttled through various houses and camps until he came, in the winter, to Turkey's west coast. He made the crossing. He was alone. Eight months later, his wife and his daughter, now seven, joined him. When he tells me that, his eyes soften for a moment. His name and theirs are tattooed one after the other, like the single jagged line of a hospital heart monitor, on the outside of his forearm.

'This sea, this ocean, it's horrible,' he says. 'But we're trying, this whole journey, for a better life, for the children. For the next generation. What can we do? Without any money, without any support from the government in the first country? The borders are, in my mentality, bullshit. Why? It's just one sea. In some places just six kilometres. Everything is changing in six kilometres.'

It wasn't always this way. For centuries Lesbos was part of the Ottoman Empire. There was a mix of faiths on the island, Muslim and Christian, as there was throughout much of the Empire, working and farming alongside one another under the Sultan's rule, mostly with tolerance and respect. Mytilene itself was seen as a model of how the religions could live together. And across the water, Greeks had been on the Anatolian coast for the past 3,000 years. Towns like Ayvalık and Smyrna, later renamed Izmir, were almost entirely Greek.

But by the early nineteenth century the model began unravelling as the more modern notion of nationalism took hold. The newly formed kingdom of Greece, explicitly Christian, declared independence from the Empire and forced the Ottoman to retreat. At the same time, as tensions rose across the region, more and more Christians left Anatolia for the Balkans. Yet things only truly collapsed at the beginning of the twentieth century. In 1912 Greece pushed east, capturing Thessaloniki and most of the Aegean islands, including Lesbos, almost doubling the size of its territory and taking charge of a large Muslim population. A decade of fighting followed. By the autumn of 1922, the Turkish army, commanded by Kemal Atatürk, had reached Turkey's west coast, driving the Greek army before it. In Smyrna, a fire in the Greek and Armenian quarters killed up to 100,000 people. In Ayvalık, the women and children fled in boats for Lesbos; of 3,000 men forced into labour battalions in Anatolia, only twenty-three survived. Many of those living in Mytilene today are the descendants of those who survived that crossing, a century ago.

Masoud Ghorbanpour is, as much as the words have meaning, one of the lucky ones. He received his residence permit: his family is allowed to stay. But the tax number which should have followed has not arrived. Each time he visits the tax office he is told to come back in two months. Without a tax number, he cannot work. He cannot rent a flat. His daughter is not enrolled in school. For now he is still in the camp with his family, living in an Isobox, and they still receive their collective monthly stipend of €190. But that is due to stop six months after receiving his residence permit, which will be any day now.

'I'm losing my mother tongue because of stress,' he says. 'I'm trying to make conversation with my wife but I can't because I'm forgetting everything. I'm forgetting the password for my phone. I have headaches, always. Backaches, needle pains in the fingers. In the left leg, in the left hand, the left arm. Neck pain. Heart pain. Stomach pain. I have to take Ritalin in the morning. Omeprazole in the evening. A lot of paracetamol with ibuprofen during the day. I have a lot of nausea, a lot of stress. My hand, my leg is shaking all the time. Really, how can I survive in this situation? I want to work. But everything is linked to my tax number.'

Migrant, from the Latin *migrare*, to move from one place to another. Not emigrant, not immigrant, not leaving or arrived, but migrant, in motion. Except the life of a migrant is not defined by motion. It is instead a life of brief shuttles between periods of interminable waiting. It is waiting in line for two hours for each meal. It is waiting in the tax office, the police station, the hospital. It is waiting for Western Union to open. It is waiting for two years for a decision on your claim. It is waiting for an identity that is something more than 'migrant'. It is waiting that is fuelling the mental health crisis that now comprises the majority of healthcare on the island, a crisis that the care here is chronically ill-equipped to manage. Last year, Médecins Sans Frontières described Moria refugee camp as an open-air 'mental asylum'.

It is the life of Masoud's daughter that concerns him most. 'I'm thirty-two,' he says. 'I'm done. But she is seven years old. They have to grow with a nice mentality. She's not something like a flower or fruit. She's a human. And I worry about the side effects in her future.' She has only an hour and a half of schooling each day, provided by one of the camp's NGOs. She is learning Greek and English, nothing else. 46 per cent of refugees on the island are children. They can expect to be here for years.

'I'm in the bubble right now,' he says. 'Greece situation, Greek rules, is a bubble for me. Right now I'm here,' and he gestures a little higher than the table where we are sitting, where our iced coffees are warming. 'But five years later, I'm *here*.' He points up into the blue of the sky. 'And if I'm coming to ground after that . . .' He tails off. 'I'm exploding if I hit the ground from there,' he says. 'If I escaped right now, it's better for me and my family.'

More than a million migrants arrived in Europe by sea in 2015. This was the year of the highly publicised deaths, the capsized boats, of Alan Kurdi face down in the sand. The words 'refugee crisis' rolled off the tongue as the news clichés do: they suggested a unique moment, a temporary aberration before everyone could settle back into their lives. And indeed, for all the horrors, passage through Europe was often relatively quick. Arrivals to Lesbos would be on boats to Athens within days, and then move north, a shifting route as borders opened and closed, as rumours spread, everyone on course for Germany, for Sweden, for Britain.

Then in March 2016, the EU–Turkey deal was signed. The agreement, forged in Brussels, spearheaded by Germany, stipulated that everyone arriving 'irregularly' on the Greek islands should be returned swiftly to Turkey. In exchange, Turkey was to receive €6 billion to deal with its already vast refugee population, and Europe would take one Syrian refugee off Turkey's hands for every Syrian that was returned to Turkey from the islands. Turkish nationals were granted visa-free travel to Europe.

Overnight, the reception centres on the islands became detention centres. The Greek government began rejecting asylum applications out of hand. And yet as of the end of July 2019, only 1,884 people have been returned to Turkey in the past three years, according to Turkey's interior ministry. Appeals drag on for years. Greek courts have ruled in many cases that Turkey is not a safe country for return. And so most people have become stuck on the islands, neither moving forward nor back, as the conditions in the Aegean become ever more squalid and overcrowded. There are currently more than

11,000 refugees on Lesbos, and Moria camp is nearly four times over capacity.

Yet the crisis, apparently, is over. In 2015, 861,630 people arrived in Greece and as of September 2019, the number is 38,598. Governments would have you believe that the situation has been brought under control. The deals, the walls, the hard-line stances, the hostile environments: all these are having an effect. But numbers can disguise an awkward human story. They do not mention the 40,000 people, including 15,000 children, who have been arrested en route and sent back to Turkey. They do not mention that 2019 has been far deadlier in the Mediterranean than 2015, as closed borders and the legal limbo on the islands push people towards ever more desperate routes, while at the same time rescue boats are prevented from carrying out their work. And they do not mention that the arrivals this August on the islands are the highest for a single month since early 2016, when the EU–Turkey deal was signed, as fears of Turkey organising mass deportations of its refugees propel thousands once more towards Europe. Six hundred came in a single day. A series of emergency measures, swiftly hammered out by the new Greek government, includes stepping up the border force and removing the right of appeal for failed asylum seekers, deporting them to their country of origin.

At least 20 per cent of the population of Anatolia died during the last ten years of the Ottoman Empire, between 1912 and 1922, as the First World War bled into the Turkish War of Independence, and the Ottoman government enacted the slaughter of its Armenian population. An estimated 2.5 million Muslims, 1.5 million Armenians, 300,000 Greeks. Nation states, with strong, unique identities, were usurping multifaith empires. For the religions to continue to cohabit seemed impossible. The Treaty of Lausanne, signed in 1923, set out a 'compulsory exchange' between Greek Orthodox Turkish nationals and Greek nationals who were Muslim. In 1923, 400,000 Muslims and 1.2 million Greek Orthodox Christians were forcibly relocated.

One million six hundred thousand people who had no connection with the land where they arrived, except that they practised the religion which was decreed by the state, were asked to believe that they were home. And yet today, Golden Dawn would have the Greek electorate believe that the arrival of Muslim refugees is diluting what it means to be Greek.

In 2019, one billion people are migrants. In 2019, the highest number of people are fleeing war since the Second World War. Should we not give these people more of a definition than one that is simply based on what they are not? Electronics and cotton sheets can cross this narrow strait with ease. And lorries parked up on the quayside in Ayvalık, await the next ferry for Europe. There is something about a person clinging to the base of a lorry that encapsulates everything about the cruel logic of free trade and impenetrable borders.

Migration will not stop: if there is a single lesson to be taken home from Lesbos it is that. To approach history with amnesia or myopia might suggest that at some point things will be back to normal, but the truth is that this is normal. The only way that 'stopping migration' makes sense is as a slogan that bolsters the far right in the creation of a perpetual drama which they are fully aware is unresolvable, a drama which peddles the lie that just as soon as an end to migration is achieved, all other problems will fade away. This slogan has so dictated the narrative that one liberal line of thought now runs that not getting tough on migration means ceding votes to the right. We must consider who these people arriving really are, and what they mean to us. Even on Lesbos, at one of the epicentres of migration, they are possible to ignore. But we cannot be neutral; this is also our story.

This year Orthodox Easter comes a week later than the Anglican. All weekend there are firecrackers in the streets, loud as gunshots, and I wonder about those sleeping in the camps and what memories the sounds stir. On the Saturday night we go down to the harbour and eat there by the water. All of Mytilene is there, it seems, dressed in their best, and when they pile out of the churches in the last of the dusk they line the harbour's streets. A cutter, gun-metal grey, is leaving for the nightly patrol, and coming the other way are all of the fishing boats, the glow of their deck lights in the dark. There is a priest leading the hymns on a loudspeaker and his low voice drifts across the water, and as the fishing boats gather, the families light the Chinese lanterns they have brought along with them. The first goes up, then several more. And all of a sudden in their hundreds they are rising into the air, their orange orbs massing above the town like the constellations set loose, piercing the night, hiding the stars. I have never seen so many. And they catch the winds up there, a stream of them being carried away off to the west, and I watch them, sitting there at my table with my family and my wine, until they fade from sight. ■

'All Europe contributed to the making of Kurtz.'
– Joseph Conrad, *Heart of Darkness*, 1902

This notorious statement, from near the end of Conrad's famous novella, still resonates to this day. Although the reality and idea of Europe is fairly credited with the absence of an all-out European war in our time, what tends to be forgotten in the evocation of Europe as bastion of freedom, culture and civilisation, is the darker history of its own colonial violence whose afterlife, its legacy of global inequality, is playing its part in the migration crisis that has fuelled – or has served to fuel – Brexit. In Conrad's story, Kurtz is the emissary of that colonial vision. Commissioned to write a report on the suppression of 'savage' customs, he is living deep in the Belgian Congo, where the narrator discovers him in the clutches of jungle frenzy, his outpost surrounded by stakes topped with the dried severed heads of murdered natives. He has gone mad, we are told, but in this extraordinary statement the narrator implies that his insanity, far from being the infectious madness of the 'uncivilised', has grown out of the very heart of European civilisation itself. Back in England, the narrator hands Kurtz's report over to the Company official, but tears off its postscript: 'Exterminate all the brutes!' Conrad could not have foreseen the genocide that would sweep across Europe in the midst of the century ushered in by his novella. Any more than he could have predicted the flight of migrants from the exploited reaches of the earth, which is today pushing parts of Europe, and not only Europe, into the hands of the far right. But, Conrad's story suggests, we will get nowhere in understanding the present crisis unless we, as Europeans, are willing to look into the dark heart of ourselves. ■

' "Distinctions of country, sacred now, may possibly disappear" in the future evolution of world society . . . he [Mazzini] holds . . . nationality must be recognised as the appointed means to international union.'
– Gwilym O. Griffith, *Mazzini: Prophet of Modern Europe*, 1932

G rowing up in Colombo in the 1960s, 'British' for me was a word found in war comics and in vague notions of an empire from which we were independent. So, 'independence' meant to be free of the 'British'. The two words were in opposition. The term 'European' referred mainly to the English (plus Scots, Welsh and Irish), and random sailors who'd been blown off course. Talk of 'Britain's independence', or 'Europe without Britain', would have seemed nonsensical babble to me then, unaware of the Pandora's box Mazzini had rattled in distant Italy a century earlier.

It was only in the 1970s that I began to see that the definition of a word could be a political project. Ceylon became a republic: Sri Lanka – with troubling questions as to who would be entitled to be its citizens. That same year, the Ugandan crisis resulted in a call to redefine British identity. Within ten years a bizarre hierarchy of nationality from born-in-Britain British to made-in-the-Commonwealth British had been established. Identity, it seemed, was not so self-determined after all. Apparently, I had been a British subject (as all Commonwealth citizens were) unwittingly in independent Ceylon, but in post-republican Sri Lanka was no longer so. When my children were born in London, they burst in undeniably British (and by extension European) and I suddenly became British too, again – identity augmented and plural much in the way I had become both son and father. To be more than one thing seemed to me to be the way to go; your position in the parade a matter of perception. ■

MY CHEQUERED EUROPE

Melitta Breznik

TRANSLATED FROM THE GERMAN BY CHARLOTTE COLLINS

M y parents gave me the wooden travel chess set for Easter, just
after my eighth birthday. Scarcely had I made my first few
attempts to play with it when I was overcome by the urge to write
my full address inside. Melitta Breznik, Winklerweg, Kapfenberg,
Styria, Austria, Europe, Earth, Solar System, Milky Way. Reading
that today, I find it a little embarrassing, but it also makes me smile.
What surprises me is the mention of Europe – a word that, back then,
was generally thought of as referring to a subcontinent. It hadn't yet
acquired the political dimension it has today. I knew from a school
trip that on the eastern horizon, which we could sense in the distance
from the top of the giant Ferris wheel in Vienna, there was a sharp
border: the Iron Curtain, with barbed wire and watchtowers, a man-
made division into Western and Eastern Europe of a region that
geographically belonged together. What would a Czech, Polish or
Latvian schoolgirl my age have written inside her travel chess set in
1969? Europe? When you took the train from Kapfenberg to Vienna
and studied the rattling departure board at the Südbahnhof, the
frontier of the Iron Curtain was imprinted on your subconscious
over and over again; because, unlike today, the only names you saw
there, in that high, gloomy hall with its 1950s charm, were those of
frontier stations on our side of the border. Nor could you escape the

art installation that hung from the ceiling on a long cable: it showed a blinking eye on a screen, and as you slowly descended the escalator from platform level to the ticket hall it emitted repetitive clicks, which could be heard at a considerable distance. The black-and-white eye didn't belong in this desolate non-place of arrivals and departures – or perhaps it did, because it referenced the way the machinery of surveillance was taken for granted, part of our daily lives, and its acoustic and visual omnipresence was unpleasantly disturbing. The Südbahnhof no longer exists; it was superseded by the Hauptbahnhof, whose functional modernity provides an emotion-free departure point for a trip to Bratislava, Budapest or Brno.

Seen from Austria, 'our Europe' also sort of included Hungary, because some of the grown-ups still went to health resorts on Lake Balaton. Croatia was kind of included because people would go to the Croatian islands for their holidays, just as their grandparents or parents had done before the collapse of the Austro-Hungarian Empire. And then of course Slovenia belonged a bit as well, because the new wine always tasted better in the southern air, in the taverns just 'over there', across the border, rather than 'over here'. Yugoslavia was always different; that border never seemed as impermeable as the one in the 'real' East. There was a Yugoslavian guest worker who lived in our workers' apartment block; on the one hand, people didn't want too much to do with him, yet everyone relied on his physical strength. He would turn over the garden for the old widow on the ground floor or heave crates of potatoes onto the lorry at the greengrocer's to earn a few extra schillings for his wife and four children in Serbia. Our family only ever mentioned in passing the fact that my grandfather had immigrated in the 1920s in search of work from what was then Lower Styria in the Austro-Hungarian Empire; Yugoslavia in the interim, now Slovenia. It was more likely to be noted that my grandfather, a skinny, taciturn man of whom I was especially fond, came from a hamlet that was called Breznik (now Brezni Vrh), as if this indicated a claim to ownership, or even a noble title of some kind. Decades later, by which time I had settled in Switzerland, I visited this hamlet while trying to trace his origins. I looked around the cemetery above Radlje in the Drava valley, asked the surrounding farmers about my grandfather and our ancestors, and was given a warm welcome. Calls were made to neighbours to gather information about 'Eduard'; food was brought and my glass filled with wine and schnapps until I could hardly stand. I felt strangely happy and at home in this community, although ultimately I didn't know if we were directly related. When I took my leave I turned to the elderly grandmother, who was wearing a traditional, brightly patterned headscarf, a standard countrywoman's accessory in south-eastern regions. All day she had simply smiled at the excitement surrounding my appearance without saying anything. To her family's surprise, she addressed a single sentence to me in crystal-clear German: 'I am very pleased that you have come to visit us.' She had spoken German as a child, but never used it later on; after the end of the First World War, when the borders were drawn more tightly around Vienna, it would no longer have been politic, as other rulers were calling the shots in the kingdom of Serbs, Croats and Slovenes that subsequently gave birth to Yugoslavia in the aftermath of the Second World War.

My mother was from Frankfurt am Main, and when I was seven years old we drove across the border to Germany to meet her friend and walk around a city that, as my mother kept saying, didn't look the way it had in her youth: wartime bombing had reduced many of the buildings to rubble. In the evening, when they thought I was asleep, I secretly listened to their stories about the fearful hours they had spent together during air raids while on Labour Service at the IG Farben factory. I heard about the air-raid warnings my mother had had to trigger at the telephone exchange before the roaring squadrons of bombers reached the city. Even today I freeze and a cold shudder runs down my spine when, at precisely midday on a Saturday in an Austrian town, the siren test slices metallically through the peaceful air. Our family's story began back then, in the Second World War, when my father, as part of his job with the communication service of the German Wehrmacht, would telephone my mother to inform her of an impending attack and instruct her to sound the sirens. Eventually, between bomb alerts, they arranged to meet and go to the cinema. Decades later, it was the ghosts that had lodged themselves in their bodies amid the din of falling bombs, exploding grenades and salvos of machine-gun fire that caused their relationship to founder. My brother and I reluctantly bore witness to these ghosts throughout our childhood. To this day I can still hear the screams of the French forced labourers, trapped in a cellar opposite my mother's workplace, who burned to death after an air raid: she told me about them over and over again.

Years later, I thought about these prisoners of war as I stood on a bridge over the Seine, watching as the sky behind the roofs of the Parisian apartment buildings was engulfed by the 'blue hour': it had an intensity I've never encountered elsewhere. It was the early 1990s, and I was in Paris for the first time. I spent a few weeks there around Christmas, whiling away the hours in the city's cafes and museums, engrossed in writing my first book. The little Parisian apartment at my disposal was on the top floor of an old town house. In my memory I see the floor of the narrow kitchen with its square black-and-white tiles, the tall, ill-fitting windows, the winding wooden staircase that led up from the hall, the fake fireplace lit by gas and above it the mirror with bevelled edges in which I can still glimpse my reflection. There in the hallway are the beige suede shoes with the high heels that gave me blisters as I walked and walked around the unfamiliar city.

When I was ten, my mother and I travelled to Piraeus with my father, who wanted to show us the places where he had been stationed in the Second World War. We languished for more than forty hours in shabby train compartments, opening the window as far as it would go to mitigate the heat and the smell of sweat emanating from our fellow passengers. The journey took us past the prefab apartments of Belgrade, which seemed monstrous to me, a resident of a small Austrian industrial town. At a leisurely pace, accompanied by a basso continuo 'ta-tam-ta-tam', we crossed never-ending green fields, followed the courses of rivers and rolled ever deeper into mountain landscapes with countless narrow, dark tunnels. I remember long stops for no apparent reason at dirty, run-down train stations; the taste of the small, exotically seasoned lamb skewers sold by countrywomen at the border with Greece, which was still, in those days, under military dictatorship. For many years, always around Easter time, my father would travel to the country where he had spent a year as a young Wehrmacht soldier. Meteora, Piraeus, Corinth – I'd grown up hearing these auspicious names, and it was on this trip with my parents that I saw the turquoise infinity of the sea for the first time. We stayed in a small, whitewashed house in the port of Athens with a Greek man and his family, who hosted us and made us welcome. He and my father had shared some sort of experience during the war that they didn't discuss when they spoke together in their broken English. A silent, amicable understanding seemed to exist between them for reasons that remained hidden to us. I was too young at the time to interrogate him about his experiences. Eventually, in later years, I stopped trying to retrace my father's footsteps – stopped researching his time in the Wehrmacht, reading descriptions of the Wehrmacht's terrible massacres in Greek villages, going through reports in English and German archives from the military units to which he was assigned. He took the secret of his friendship, perhaps also of his guilt, to the grave.

From the age of twelve onwards, England became increasingly familiar to me. My school friend's mother was from London. She made curry with chutney for lunch, and at five in the afternoon she served biscuits and delicious English tea, the function of which I only came to appreciate much later, when preparing for my anatomy and pathology exams: it kept me awake over my books until late into the night. I often stayed over with my 'English friend'; I would stand outside her front door, carrying a little rucksack stuffed with my nightdress, schoolbooks, and vegetables from our allotment, waiting for her to let me in so I could immerse myself in another kind of life: the 'English' life of her home. We would spend long afternoons in her room, listening to the Beatles or Simon & Garfunkel, learning the lyrics by heart and singing them in our thin, girlish voices. Both of us were juniors at the academic secondary school; we used to rehearse little sketches and perform them in English class the following day.

A few years ago, I spent six months in London on a literature scholarship. My original intention was to work on my novel, but I was too distracted by my walks around the city. On a sudden impulse, I started researching the time my father had spent in a prisoner-of-war camp, and finally found what I was looking for in Romsey, in southern England. I contacted the local historical society, and a friendly elderly lady said she would be available to give me a guided tour. My father was there for two years, and in the months before his release he had been assigned to work on a farm near the camp. My mother once voiced a suspicion that we might have a half-brother or -sister in England.

At sixteen I put my name down at school to spend a year abroad, and was accepted. My three fellow pupils who applied at the same time all wanted to go to the United States, but my parents refused to allow me to travel across the Atlantic. So I had no option but to sign up for the Europe programme, although you couldn't choose the country where you were to spend twelve months living with a host family. I hoped I could go to France, as I enjoyed the language and wanted to use the opportunity to immerse myself more fully in the culture. Then a letter arrived with a photo of a family near Stavanger, Norway. At first I was disappointed, but my initial scepticism gave way to impatient curiosity. Setting off for my year abroad, I watched the Vienna Airport terminal building shrink beneath me and imagined my parents standing silently together, gazing upwards, until the dot on the horizon disappeared. Much later, as my mother lay dying, I sat beside her singing Norwegian folk songs, quietly and solemnly, in a minor key, in what had become my second language – songs I had learned during my time at school there. Norway and my Norwegian host family are still part of my life today.

Then there was Italian, the language that, in its playful luminosity, felt like a liberation to me after eight years of Latin at school: the endless translation exercises from Caesar's *De Bello Gallico* and Ovid's *Metamorphoses* that often threatened to crush and stifle me. Even in the secure unit of the psychiatric hospital near Milan, where I was a visiting student for a few weeks, the sound of Italian conveyed to me a cheerful warmth that can sometimes feel exaggerated to Central Europeans. Nothing could be more agreeable than sitting around the table at my friend's house in Pavia for lunch, listening to her two adolescent daughters discussing Italy's membership of the European Community, and how this would hasten the demise of the Mafia, over a warm salad of octopus with celery and potatoes. Then there were the many drives to Milan or Florence, crossing the border from Innsbruck to South Tyrol, where the Italian border guards with machine guns at the ready always gave an ambivalent impression. It was as if they didn't take their uniforms, which I thought were rather over the top, terribly seriously, but were acting in a nationwide play. In my boundless naivety, or perhaps this was just a young person's tendency to overlook boundaries, I once had my dog, a clumsy Leonberger, in the car with me on the way back from Italy. The Austrian border guard made me get out and explained to me in no uncertain terms that I had to declare the puppy or it would be impounded on the spot. When I'd entered Austria two weeks earlier after collecting it from the German breeder near Freiburg im Breisgau, I had forgotten to import it officially via customs. It was therefore still a 'German dog'.

I can't recall when exactly the first visible preparations for European membership began in our provincial Austrian town, but suddenly there were activities taking place at every level. German, French and Italian choirs were invited to visit and marched through the old town in traditional costume, place-name signs were diligently swapped, the name of a twin town was added, the European flag raised. When a stretch of road was renamed Europe Square in a town where, alongside the usual Austrian designations, most squares and streets were named after local Schutzbund fighters who had been killed or executed in the Austrian Civil War, it was the start of a new era. Kolomann Wallisch Square, Josef Stanek Street – for me, these names acquired faces only later on, when I went looking for evidence of my grandfather's involvement in the 1934 workers' uprising in Kapfenberg against the proto-fascist dictatorship of Dollfuss's Christian Social Party. My grandfather was lucky: he wasn't caught, and didn't have to flee across the border from Austria to Czechoslovakia like many other Republican fighters who were smuggled into the Soviet Union by the Workers' International Relief. Later, during the Second World War, German speakers were persecuted, deported or murdered in the Soviet Union. I can imagine that when the Austrian army finally moved in and the Schutzbund fighters' situation became desperate, my grandfather just cycled away. Thirty-four years later he taught me to ride a bike in the backyard of the block of workers' apartments where I grew up: it was his old Puch Waffenrad, the same bike he had used to retreat from the fighting.

Suddenly, with the Schengen Agreement, there were no border controls any more, no stopping and searching for your (hopefully still valid) passport, no penetrating looks from customs officers. It still horrifies me to recall a drive across East Germany in the late 1980s. Heading to Scandinavia during the university summer break, a friend and I hitched a lift in a lorry. Stopping at a grotesquely fortified border to cross into this country that both was and wasn't Germany; the armed, uniformed men with their cold faces, the submissive Alsatians at their side – I still find even the memory of it oppressive. Years later, I crossed the border between Slovenia and Croatia during the war in Yugoslavia. I didn't know I would be stopped a few kilometres further on, at four in the morning, by martial-looking figures in makeshift camouflage uniforms manning an improvised checkpoint on a cross-country road in Istria – the route to Lovran, an old imperial Austro-Hungarian spa resort. In my mind, the familiarity of the name Lovran rendered the destination harmless. But there was still fighting in the south of the country; there was still a war on, being waged by means that were very far from fair.

These, then, are the borders with which I grew up and have spent a part of my life: in a Europe of small constituent parts, a Europe whose history has, for centuries, been defined by shifting borders and the wars that have been fought over them. A Europe of different languages, landscapes and cultures, all of which have retained their characters. But some things have changed, too; some have disappeared, while other, new things have come into being. More freedoms are now taken for granted. I will go on making friends and maintaining friendships across national and linguistic borders; my travel chess set will continue to accompany me as I drive along German, French, Italian, Greek, Belgian, Dutch, Danish, Slovenian, Croatian, Czech, Norwegian and English roads, and I will endeavour to acquaint myself with the remaining parts of Europe where I have not yet travelled.

I have no memory of border controls in England before the existence of the European Union. By the time you boarded the ferry, you had already crossed to another country. The emergence of the white chalk cliffs was the most impressive natural border imaginable, rising up majestically in the morning mist, more a greeting than a deterrent. I would be astonished if I were now to be met at the foot of the cliffs by uniformed border police. ∎

'What times are these, in which
A conversation about trees is almost a crime
For in doing so we maintain our silence about so much wrongdoing!'
– Bertolt Brecht, 'An die Nachgeborenen', 1939, translated from the German
by Scott Horton

'An die Nachgeborenen' was a dark prophecy of collapsing Europe, when many people – those who were not slaughtered on the battlefields or killed in concentration camps – changed countries more frequently than shoes. Including Brecht himself, who wrote these verses in Danish exile in 1939.

Today, as right-wing populism and xenophobia, border fortifications and refugees are rising once again across Europe and the world, Brecht's words reverberate like poetic thunder from the future.

We are the *Nachgeborenen*, born after the horrors of the Second World War. We are the ones who are responsible for not repeating the mistakes of the past.

When thousands of refugees are drowning in the graveyard of the Mediterranean, and millions of others are displaced, how can we still be talking about trees?

But what if the only way out of our current dark times is to turn Brecht's lines around? What if, given the disastrous effects of climate crisis – ravaging wildfires, water shortages, record-breaking temperatures – it is not a crime to speak about trees any more, but precisely the opposite: a duty in order to save Europe and the world from itself?

Truly, we live in dark times. But if we are not talking about trees, we are not talking about the radical and profound changes we need, not only in politics and economics, but more broadly in the way we treat the Other and Nature itself. We need to talk about trees if we are to talk about survival. ■

'Our Europe is a shared adventure which we will continue to pursue, despite you, in the wind of intelligence.'
– Albert Camus, *Letters to a German Friend*, 1944

'The wind of intelligence.' I like expressions like this. You never hear them in politicians' speeches. They only find their place in literature. And yet these are the words we need, the ones that can fill us with élan and enthusiasm.

Fervent social awareness and civic passion have deserted today's Europe. It bores its own citizens. We need wind, great gusts of ideas, to dust off old habits and uplift hearts. Wind, yes, so that we will not forget that in the early days of European construction, there was a utopian idea: to ensure that countries which, in the past, were so often rivals, so often enemies, would bind their fates to one another.

When Camus wrote these words, the Second World War was not yet over. He had gone underground, and was fighting. He wrote these words in order to propose a counterplan against dictatorship and the Nazi domination of Europe. He wrote them to give himself a compass. The wind of intelligence is what defines us: an open, humanist culture in motion, the heir to a victorious struggle against criminal dogma.

Literature has its role to play in this adventure. Literature has the right to be angry, passionate, or euphoric; lyrical or epic. Literature alone holds the secret key to enthusiasm. Let us produce texts that will be more than just critical, more than just cautious. There is nothing to stop us from celebrating, exploring further, shouting louder; nothing to stop us from dreaming of impossible countries that we will make into reality. There is nothing to stop us from taking the wind for our banner. ■

Translated from the French by Alison Anderson

The author's grandmother and great-grandmother
Courtesy of the author

EXILE

Elif Shafak

'Exile is the fate of the contemporary poet, regardless of
whether he lives in his native land or abroad, because he
is almost always torn away from the little familiar world
of customs and beliefs that he knew in his childhood.'
– Czesław Miłosz, *The Land of Ulro,* translated from the
Polish by Louis Iribarne

The first time I heard the word exile – *sürgün* – in Turkish, I
was a child. It struck me how closely it rhymed with another
word: *hüzün* – melancholy. I was seven years old and had just started
primary school in Ankara. Our house was in a deeply patriarchal,
conservative neighbourhood. Having arrived here from France, and
unable to keep pace with the other children, I often felt misplaced,
different, *weird.*

I was born in Strasbourg. A small flat in a tower block full of leftist
students, immigrants, reading Fanon and Althusser, smoking strong
tobacco, mostly Gauloises. Not long after, my parents' marriage came
to an end. My father stayed in France and got married again while my
mother brought me to Ankara, to Grandma's house. For my mother,
Turkey was 'the motherland', the country where we belonged. For me,
it was a new place altogether, one that I had to discover on my own.

Thus we arrived in Grandma's universe. Two-storey houses, small gardens with cherry trees, aromas of fried eggplants and garlicky yogurt and dried apples, evil-eye beads, invisible djinn dancing around after sunset . . . A twilight world. All the other children in the vicinity came from large, extended families with fathers as the heads of the households, whereas I was raised by two women. Once a boy called me 'bastard' to my face and I remember the word did not hurt me, for I had no idea what it meant, but the coldness of his tone pierced me.

My grandmother and my mother were as different as night and day, or a tavern and a mosque. Mum is secular, modern, rational, urban and very fond of written culture. She passed on to me the love of books. Grandma was spiritual, highly irrational and yet remarkably wise. She was fond of oral culture – legends, myths, folk tales. She taught me to listen carefully to stories – but also to silences.

By the time I started primary school, it was the moral teachings of these two women that I carried with me when I walked into a classroom of forty-three children. The teacher – a tall, sinewy and strict woman with perfectly manicured fingernails and a wooden ruler she did not hesitate to put to use when someone misbehaved – wasn't pleased to learn that I was left-handed.

'Every year there are one or two,' she said. 'Don't worry. We'll take care of it.'

It was common practice back then. Left-handed children had to be *corrected*. There was another student in the classroom who, although seemingly in the same boat as me, was able to make the transition without a hitch. He was ambidextrous. I was not. I found it extremely hard to write with my right hand, and perhaps, just perhaps, something in me kept resisting.

'It's not working,' the teacher said one day in the middle of spring. She looked tired and somehow older. I knew she was disappointed in me. 'There is no other way. We must send your left hand into exile.'

'Where?' I asked anxiously. Here was another word I had never heard before.

'Yes we must.' She nodded her head, agreeing with herself. 'We'll pretend your left hand has gone to another country.'

I was flabbergasted. How could one part of me be *somewhere else* while the rest of me was *here*? How could I be whole if I remained divided?

'Until you have fully learned to make good use of your right hand,' the teacher carried on, as if sensing my confusion. 'Afterwards your left hand can return.'

Thus I was instructed to keep my left hand under the desk at all times. During class hours, my *sinful* hand would remain banished. Meanwhile, I would do everything with my right hand, my *good* hand – holding a pencil, opening a book, asking permission to speak . . .

This is how I came to learn that the world under the desk was the *Land of Exile*. Dusty, dark, unwanted. A place of rejection, punishment and forsakenness. Once something was sent into exile, you did not have to think about it much. It was out of sight, out of mind.

After a full year of repeated failures and a few detentions, I was able to learn how to write with my right hand and my right hand only. And years later, as a novelist who has always been dependent on all kinds of typewriters, computers and laptops, I hate my own handwriting and feel uncomfortable if I have to hold a pencil or a pen for longer than a few minutes. Today, when readers ask me to sign their books, I am happy to do that, but I cannot help murmuring apologies every now and then for my illegible handwriting.

Turkey has a long history of sending its writers and poets into exile. This tradition, if that's what it is, goes all the way back to the Ottoman Empire. Every poet, novelist, academic or intellectual today knows that words are loaded. Because of a poem, a novel, an article, a sentence uttered in an interview or even a retweet, one can get into trouble overnight. The next day you may wake up to pro-government papers branding you a 'traitor' and trolls on social media bombarding you with insults and slander. In only a matter of hours you can be sued, arrested, sacked or exiled. We all know this: there is, therefore, widespread self-censorship among writers.

Osman Kavala, a leading philanthropist and businessman, and one of the most gentle souls and kindest people I have ever known, is still being held unlawfully in jail. Ahmet Altan, the novelist and journalist, has been sentenced to life in prison. Selahattin Demirtaş, the leader of the majority-Kurdish political party HDP, is in jail, his voice silenced. In 2018 alone, 113,000 Turks left Turkey.

Since my childhood, life has always been nomadic. Besides Ankara I have lived in Madrid, Amman and Cologne. Then, in my early twenties, I moved to Istanbul on my own. I did not know a single soul and I did not have a job, but I strongly believed that the city was calling me and that it was here that I should write my novels. For years, I studied Istanbul's history, questioned its collective amnesia, roamed its side streets and alleys, recorded its graffiti, researched its nooks and crannies, tried to give a voice to its untold stories. I fell in love with Istanbul. But she was a difficult lover, and always has been. Feeling suffocated, I went to Boston, Michigan and Arizona. Later, I returned to Istanbul, and continued to write and publish here. But things did not get easier. After I wrote *The Bastard of Istanbul* in 2006, there were ultra-nationalist mobs on the streets burning my photograph next to the EU flag. My novel focused on two families, one Turkish, the other Armenian-American, telling the painful stories of the Armenian genocide through the eyes of generations of women. I was put on trial for 'insulting Turkishness' under Article 301. My Turkish lawyer had to defend my Armenian fictional characters in the courtroom and for two years I lived with a bodyguard. Today my fiction is once again being scrutinised by the authorities, this time for the 'crime of obscenity' – for writing about issues such as sexual harassment, child abuse and gender-based violence.

About ten years ago, I uprooted myself once again and moved to London. Self-imposed exile is hard to explain to yourself, let alone to others. It does involve a geographical displacement, a physical separation from language, culture, *familiarity*. But more than that it is a feeling you cannot shed: a sense of being only partly present.

My grandmother passed away recently. I could not attend her funeral. I did not feel comfortable travelling to Turkey at a time when academics, journalists and writers were being arrested or targeted on the most baseless of charges. I did not want to talk about this either. It didn't seem right to even mention it when so many other people were going through enormous difficulties and injustices. And yet I have carried this sense of separation from Istanbul within me for so long now that it surfaces involuntarily sometimes, when I hear a song or miss the taste of fried mussels, the sound of a seagull's cry, the smell of the salty wind.

Friends who travel back and forth ask me sometimes if there is anything I would like them to bring. This I don't say. But I wish they could bring me my coffee-stained copy of Walter Benjamin's *The Arcades Project*, left on a wooden bench on the upper deck of a ferry boat zigzagging between the islands. I'd like to believe that it is still there, its pages turning in the breeze. But I know the book is not there any more: that moment in time is gone, and so is, perhaps, the country that I used to know and call home. ■

Russian author Anton Chekhov (1860–1904), bottom right, with his friends and family at his house in Moscow

ON THE ISLAND OF
THE BLACK RIVER

William Atkins

'I ordinarily answer such as ask me the reason for my
travels, "that I know very well what I fly from, but not
what I seek." ' – Michel de Montaigne, translated from
the French by Charles Cotton

1

In 1890 Anton Chekhov took an axe to his life. He went to the
prison island of Sakhalin, more than 4,000 miles from his home
in Moscow. The journey took him eleven weeks by road, river and
sea. His three months on the island were spent mainly in the capital,
Alexandrovsk, interviewing convicts and former convicts, voluntary
exiles, administrators and prison overseers. The resulting description
of squalor, mass sexual abuse, incompetence and systemic cruelty
at the far edge of the empire would become a cause célèbre back in
European Russia when it was serialised, then published as a book, three
years later, and lead to a secret government inquiry into the running
of the penal colony. 'I regret that I am not a sentimental person,' he
told his publisher before he left, 'otherwise I would say that we should
make pilgrimages to places like Sakhalin as Turks go to Mecca.'

At the derelict harbour in Alexandrovsk, as I was taking a photo
of a plaque commemorating his arrival on the island, there was a pain

in my calf so deep and startling that I was caught, like Buridan's ass, between shrieking and puking, and instead ceased, for a while, to breathe. It was my fault: the dog had been barking from its lookout of rubble with that squint-eyed ripping motion of serious dogs, and I'd turned away. It did its job so well that all memory of its appearance has gone – big or small; what breed or colour. I took off my sock and tied it around the wound and, my shoe slopping with blood, flagged down a car.

Pushing the needle into my back an hour later, the nurse said, 'Now you have something to write about, don't you?' The doctor battled an undoctorly smirk while jotting down his notes.

I went back to the town's solitary hotel, the Three Brothers, shook the blood from my shoe into the toilet, swallowed some antibiotics and went to bed. Next morning, when I was told that a minor earthquake had struck while I was sleeping, it didn't come as a surprise, and not only because Sakhalin lies in a region of seismic unrest.

2

In Moscow a week earlier the intersections around Red Square were blocked by orange municipal dump trucks; bullet-vested police were guarding the approaches and by 9 a.m. bands of bearded young proto-Cossacks were standing in circles roaring battle songs into the sky. It was Victory Day, celebrating the surrender of Nazi Germany, and later President Putin would be addressing the troops. By design or accident, an international a cappella festival was on at the same time. The outdoor stages were set up in the same squares as makeshift screens playing looped war footage, so that the singers' earnest harmonising – a beatbox version of 'Superstition', for instance – vied for your attention with, say, the Red Army Choir doing 'Arise, Great Country', reaching an equilibrium of volume that became intolerable until the a cappella people hit the chorus.

On Pushkin Square 300 members of the Moscow Communist Interbrigade were carrying flags bearing the hammer and sickle and

Lenin's face. Among them was a green flag with another stencilled likeness – Che? No, Gaddafi. '*Net kapitalizmu! Net fashizmu!*' a man was chanting into a loudhailer. Over the heads of the crowd it was possible to glimpse, beyond the barricades, a ballistic missile as big as a grain silo creeping down Tverskaya towards Red Square.

Meanwhile, a mile away, Putin was mid-speech: 'Our nation is well aware of what war is. It brought grief and immeasurable suffering to every family. We have not forgotten anything. We remember everything . . .'

But the past wasn't for everyone. In the bars of Kitay Gorod half the women seemed to be wearing the same brand of denim trench coat, printed across the back: 'Good things come to those who hustle'.

In the Pushkin State Museum of Fine Arts I lingered over Lucas Cranach the Elder's *The Fall of Man*: Adam and Eve as pale and delicate as rhizomes, about to be kicked out of the Garden of Eden. No longer innocent, maybe, but they can't really comprehend what their new life will be like.

Chekhov's house on Sadovaya-Kudrinskaya Street, now a museum, was closed for refurbishment. There's a famous photo of him taken on the veranda just before he left for Sakhalin in spring 1890. He's barely thirty, surrounded by family and friends. They're all dressed in black except Anton Pavlovich, who is wearing a cream overcoat. He's raring to go; you can see it. It is an image of love and pride, the special son; and an image of all he was abandoning.

3

Although Siberia had been a place of banishment for Russia since the 1600s, in the late nineteenth century the number of criminals and political exiles sent to its penal-labour sites became unsustainable. By 1876 some 20,000 convicts were arriving each year. Prisoners were dying of exposure, malnutrition and disease. Escapes and crime soared, and there was insufficient labour to occupy those who remained. According to one visiting ethnographer, the region resembled a 'battlefield'. A large, sparsely populated, coal-rich island in the far east promised to serve the dual purpose of relieving the pressure on Siberia and consolidating the Russian frontier. Writing to his sceptical publisher, Aleksey Suvorin, a few weeks before he left, Chekhov explained that 'Sakhalin is the only place, except for Australia in former times, and Cayenne, where one can study a place that has been colonised by convicts'.

At more than 28,000 square miles, almost as big as Austria, Sakhalin is Russia's largest island. It sits in the Sea of Okhotsk opposite the Amur River delta, separated from the Russian mainland by less than five miles at its closest, its southernmost tip twenty-eight miles north of Hokkaido, Japan. It is not a St Helena in its remoteness. But by the time Chekhov arrived in summer 1890, it was already notorious. According to contemporary commentators, it was 'the final destination of the unshot [and] the unhanged', a 'land of moral darkness and abject misery'. To Suvorin, who was not persuaded of the subject's urgency, Chekhov wrote, 'Sakhalin may be uninteresting . . . only for a society which does not exile thousands of people there and does not spend millions on it . . . we have driven people tens of thousands of *versts* through the cold in shackles, infected them with syphilis, perverted them [and] multiplied the number of criminals.'

What drew him to make that interminable journey from his world's centre to its furthermost edge? Are there clues in his biography? A year before he set out, his brother Nikolay had died from tuberculosis, and Dr Chekhov was now periodically coughing up blood himself (he too had tuberculosis). He must have realised that such a demanding journey, three months of snow and mud, might kill him. His farce *The Bear* had been a triumph; his story 'The Steppe' had won the Pushkin Prize. He was known and admired. But he had been stung by criticism that his work lacked political conviction. 'Sakhalin is a place of unbearable suffering,' he told Suvorin, 'on a scale of which no creature but man is capable.' Here was a project. Finally, according to her memoirs, there was Lidiya Avilova – married, twenty-four-year-old Lidiya, with whom he may or may not have been in love.

The conflation of quest and flight is so common among travellers as to be a cliché, but I felt there was more to his decision than either grief or escapism, or a compulsion to bear witness. Look at the photo taken in the relative warmth of Moscow in April. You would not know he is sick. You wouldn't know that something is drawing him to coldness.

9 May being also the feast day of St Nicholas, patron saint of travellers, I went and lit a candle in the Cathedral of the Assumption – for the journey ahead and for my father, 1,600 miles away. At Christmas he had started a course of intensive radiotherapy. In March he had first one heart attack, then another; then pneumonia and a suspected stroke. There had been a week when we expected him to die. Now he was in hospital, unrecognisably frail, and delirious. I persuaded myself that nowhere was far away, any more. My siblings were nearby, and even on Sakhalin Island, at the 'end of the world', as Chekhov described it, I could be back within forty-eight hours. But whenever I paused, my thoughts returned to him, in his windowless ward, which one evening, hallucinating, he believed was the hold of a ship in which he had been imprisoned.

4

'The Siberian highway is the longest, and, I should think, the ugliest road on earth.' Soon after setting out, Chekhov believed he was about to die. His carriage collided with a mail troika. Thrown to the ground, he was almost run down by a second troika, which stopped just in time. In Nikolayevsk on the Amur River he boarded a steamer bound for the Tatar Strait. It was 9 July 1890. On board were some 300 soldiers and several convicts, one of whom 'was accompanied by his five-year-old daughter, who held on to his shackles as he climbed up the ship's ladder'.

From the city of Khabarovsk, almost 500 miles upstream from Nikolayevsk, I took a train to Vanino on the Tatar Strait, a journey of 300 miles and twenty-four hours. At Vanino I waited at the station to be summoned to the overnight ferry to Sakhalin. I drank pre-sugared Nescafé, watched the coal barges discharging and talked to the other waiting passengers, all of them men: a teacher from Khabarovsk, an electrician from Uzbekistan, a lighting specialist from Vladivostok, two Chinese platelayers. No one knew what time the ferry would leave.

'*Allahu Akbar*, money-money-money, fuck you, fight you . . .'

The muttering giant was coming home from South Korea; he wouldn't say what his job was but his duffel bag was military. He was sitting opposite me, glowering at the Uzbek guy. He despised Muslims. Returning from a cigarette, he toed the Uzbek's parcels: 'Bomb.' And grinned. 'Bomb!' The Uzbek looked down at his parcels and smiled tightly. People were standing up. The bus to the jetty was here.

'Perhaps I won't get anything at all from the trip,' Chekhov had told Suvorin, 'but surely to goodness there will be two or three days which I shall remember for the rest of my life, whether delightful or painful.'

5

His ship, the *Baikal*, entered the Tatar Strait on 8 July 1890, almost three months after he had left Moscow. It was a warm, bright day. 'The soul is overcome by the same feeling that Odysseus must have experienced when he sailed across an unknown sea and had a dim presentiment of meetings with extraordinary creatures.'

So narrow is the body of water between Sakhalin's Cape Pogibi and Lazarev on the mainland that until 1855 even the neighbouring Japanese believed Sakhalin was a peninsula, despite the insistence of the island's Indigenous people that it was surrounded by water. (When in 1822 an English map-maker, John Arrowsmith, showed it as an island, one eminent orientalist called him 'the most ignorant of those whose occupation is cartography'.) Northern Sakhalin's largest Indigenous group, the Nivkh, believe that the god of thunder lives beneath the sea between Pogibi and Lazarev, and so it came as no surprise to them when a tunnel ordered by Stalin collapsed during construction and was abandoned. (Putin has commissioned designs for a bridge at the strait, inspired by the one he built between Crimea and Russia in 2018.)

The ship that would take me to Kholmsk, the *Sakhalin-8*, was a rust-striped ro-ro used mainly for freight. The stink – burnt diesel oil, tobacco, garlic, reboiled sausage. (The garlic smell, it turned out, was phosphine rat poison.)

The one meal served during the fourteen-hour journey was trayed up during a half-hour slot just after we departed: buckwheat kasha, latex sausage, tea. In one corner of the galley, onions were growing in a bucket.

On deck Evgeni, engineer third class, was taking his cigarette break. He was thirty-one. I was the first native English speaker he'd met; he'd learned the language at what he called 'river school'.

'Are the English scared of the Russians?'

'The government, yes. The people, no.'

The deck door opened and a dog, a Pomeranian, was pushed out, the door closing behind it. It looked at the door, then at Evgeni and me.

Somehow Evgeni knew I was a writer. He or someone else had checked the manifest and googled the foreign name. I asked him if the *Sakhalin-8* was a good ship. He smiled and shook his head, seeing that I knew the answer. 'It is very old. From the USSR.'

To port there was a small splash – there were grey whales in these waters – then another; and I watched a plastic kettle float by . . . Another splash – what looked like a washing-machine door . . . 'Trash!' said Evgeni, as a flotilla of smaller objects bobbed past.

Evgeni showed me his phone – pictures on WhatsApp of captured Syrian armoured cars passing through his home city of Rostov on a train. Another of him gangster-posing with a Makarov pistol. He completed his army service six years ago. Did he enjoy it? He asked me to repeat the question. '*Enjoy?*' he said. 'No! Boys don't like the army! Boys like home.'

My cabin, buried three decks down, was a cornerless bunker low in the bow and resembling the interior of a tank. Against the hull there was the intermittent swash of water.

The journey to Sakhalin for most convicts was entirely by sea. Just over a year before Chekhov set out, a young Ukrainian named Lev Shternberg underwent the two-month voyage from Odessa. Born into a devout Jewish family in Zhitomir, central Ukraine, in 1861, Shternberg was just fifteen months younger than Chekhov. As a teenager he organised gatherings where he and his friends 'noisily discussed the burning issues of the day'. He read Darwin and Heine, Belinsky and Dobrolyubov and Marx. By the time he finished high school he was a staunch socialist, and when the populist movement Narodnik, then sweeping Russia, underwent a schism, he was drawn to the more radical, violent faction, Narodnaya Volya (People's Will), which was dedicated to the socialist overthrow of the government. In 1881, the year he entered the physics and mathematics department of St Petersburg University, the city was shaken by Narodnaya Volya's assassination of Alexander II. Shternberg, who had not been directly involved, was nevertheless fortunate to escape the crackdown against dissent that followed, which included the mass arrest of his Narodnaya Volya associates, many of whom were banished to Siberia. Far from heralding a new socialist republic, the assassination prompted an increase in state repression, while the peasantry the assassins had hoped to inflame into revolution instead turned against the Jewish minority it blamed for the killing. Furthermore, under emergency laws instituted by Alexander III, anyone so much as suspected of sedition was exiled to Siberia.

In 1884, undaunted, Shternberg published a pamphlet entitled 'Political Terror in Russia': the intelligentsia, he wrote, must 'use all the means available to it to overthrow the tsarist government'. Three years later, as editor of Narodnaya Volya's newsletter, Shternberg was finally arrested and imprisoned in Odessa for two years, before being sentenced, without trial, to ten years on Sakhalin. His ship, the *Petersburg*, left Odessa on 29 March 1889.

Crossing the Black Sea, it navigated the Suez Canal to Aden, before sailing on to Colombo, Singapore, Nagasaki and Vladivostok.

An observer on the same ship wrote that the journey 'recalled the most terrible scenes of Dante's *Inferno* . . . storms at sea, heat under the tropics, cold in the North Pacific [and] dirt surpassing anything the most vivid imagination could picture'. Unlike many of his fellow Populists, Shternberg never repudiated religion – the prophets were his inspiration. The voyage to Sakhalin seems to have intensified his faith. When the *Petersburg* docked at Port Said, he noticed the date on a newspaper: tomorrow was Passover. Gazing at the mountains of Sinai, he understood his plight as the perennial plight of his people; crossing the sea that the Israelites had crossed, he saw himself as one 'who also sought freedom':

> freedom not for his own people but for another people dear to him. This descendant was now destined to make a great journey, not to the Promised Land, but to the land of exile, thousands of miles away . . . And suddenly sadness disappeared from my soul and a new feeling overcame me, a feeling of pride . . . It seemed to me that a great fire had ignited in my heart, so that if millions of my dispersed brothers were with me at the moment, I would have had enough strength to use my fiery words to burn away from their hearts all impurities brought into them by centuries of oppression and slavery, and ignite a new fire in them, which would have lifted them up to the highest ideals of mankind.

He finally reached Sakhalin on 19 May 1889.

Shternberg's fate, and the transmutative effect of his exile, were a reminder that Chekhov, for all his courage, was a tourist. Nobody had invited him, still less compelled him. Indeed, until Chekhov reached Alexandrovsk he remained uncertain that he would even be granted permission to land. 'Just why did I come here?' he asks himself. 'My journey appeared frivolous in the extreme.'

I lay in my cabin, with the light on, and remembered the night when my father thought the oncology ward was a ship's hold, rusted, dripping, booming.

At 4 a.m. I was shaken awake by someone banging at my door.

6

Sakhalin is often described as sturgeon-shaped, and it does resemble a fish, a long, slender, bony fish, with two peninsulas in the south forming a forked tail, and another, resembling a dorsal fin, extending eastward into the Sea of Okhotsk. The southern half of the island is mountainous, dominated by two parallel chains, the Eastern Sakhalin Range and the Western Sakhalin Range, separated by the floodplains of the island's two rivers, rivers that somehow seem too great for the land mass they drain: the Tym, which flows north-east, and the Poronai, which flows south. The north is flatter, wetter, barer, colder and windier, mostly bog, tundra and open taiga, its coastline a scalloped lattice of lagoons. Off the north-eastern shore lie the vast oil and gas fields of the Sea of Okhotsk shelf. Alexandrovsk-Sakhalinsky, Chekhov's 'Alexandrovsk', lies halfway up the western coast, where the mountainous south meets the boggy north.

It's hard to imagine the fear and contempt the word Sakhalin conjured among the populace of tsarist Russia. According to a visitor writing in 1903, 'the very name of the island is banned in St Petersburg'. Not so much a Guantánamo as a black site. 'God is high in the sky, and the tsar is far away,' went the Siberian saying, but here both entities alike were as nothing.

When the first convicts landed at Alexandrovsk in the early 1860s, south Sakhalin, then known as Karafuto, was under Japanese control. Only when Japan ceded its territory to Russia in 1875 did the authorities start sending criminals in large numbers. By 1888 it was the largest penal settlement in Siberia. Any man sentenced to more than two years and eight months, for any crime, could be sent there, as could any woman under forty serving more than two years.

As well as common criminals and a handful of political deportees, there were three further categories on Sakhalin. 'Settled exiles' had completed their sentence but were obliged to remain on the island. After six to ten years they became 'peasants-in-exile', free to leave provided they did not return to European Russia. Thirdly, there were those who had come to the island voluntarily. 'The clever are brought here,' went an island saying; 'the idiots come on their own.' Among the 'free' were the wives of convicts, many of whom were enticed by letters from their husbands describing a land of warmth, fertility and opportunity. By the time of Chekhov's visit there were some 6,000 penal labourers on the island and 4,000 'settled exiles', most of them living in and around Alexandrovsk and the southern port of Korsakovsk.

Because Sakhalin's roads are mires in winter and rutted dust bowls in summer, it's best to travel by air or rail. My train pulled into the town of Tymovsk, fifty miles east of Alexandrovsk, just after dawn on 13 May. When I had left the modern-day capital of Yuzhno-Sakhalinsk the previous evening, the train had passed through sidings thick with fresh young bamboo (Japan is barely a hundred miles south of Yuzhno) and the birch taiga had been coming into green: in the dark of the forests, the young leaves were as bright as the spots of light from a glitterball. But as we drew into Tymovsk, 270 miles north, there was little colour and the ditches were still packed with snow.

I was met by Alexander, a driver sent by the director of the Chekhov Museum, Temur Georgiyevich Miromanov, who was also the town's former mayor. My contacts in Yuzhno-Sakhalinsk had mentioned Miromanov's intellect; they also admitted that he scared them. It was unclear if he was directly employed by the federal security services. On the ferry there had been a thin, grey-faced man in an oversized black suit, whom I became convinced was watching me; there were the two young men who sat in on my meeting at a museum in Nogliki, unintroduced and thumbing their phones as I spoke; then there was the translator who, sitting down on the sofa in my hotel room in Yuzhno, looked up at the light fittings and the smoke alarm and waved and said, not quite joking, 'Hi, guys!'

The road to Alexandrovsk rolled through taiga swamped with snowmelt. Water flowed everywhere. It was as if the island had just been winched out of the sea. Around the borders of the forest bogs were the blooms of Asian skunk cabbage. Alexander let out a flurry of grunts and squeals – it took me a moment to realise he meant the plant was used as pig fodder. Its white spathes, resembling arums, were flame-like or jug-like or like hands in benediction, rising out of the anaerobic black in groupings that seemed to correspond to the clustering patterns of anxious human crowds.

We stopped for a smoke at a churned-up field where victims of Stalin's purges had been shot and buried, hundreds of them. From the hills the road followed the streams seaward through tiers of neat white housing blocks. The road changed from dirt to asphalt. On the town square, where the prison used to be, between the house of culture and the Three Brothers hotel, in pride of place, was a bust of Chekhov.

7

N atalia was a retired English teacher who had lived in Alexandrovsk all her life. She was worried I'd have a poor opinion of her town, of her country; that I would find the hotel, the canteen, the roads uncomfortable. We walked to Alexandrovsk's fenced-off harbour, with its thickets of knotweed and angelica and its grounded and half-sunk trawlers. When the *Baikal* anchored offshore on the evening of 10 July 1890, the hills surrounding the town were aflame. 'Through the darkness and smoke spreading over the sea,' wrote Chekhov, 'I could not see the landing stage or buildings and could make out only the dim lights of the post, two of which were red . . . it looked as if the whole of Sakhalin were ablaze.' He did not need to add that it was 'as if we were in hell'.

Lev Shternberg's initial impression of the island, fourteen months earlier, was more positive: he was met by the 'courteous' district head, who explained that, as a political exile, he would be granted an allowance, spared hard labour and permitted to take paid office work. However, he wrote to a friend, 'my own privileged position does not make it easier to watch the suffering of people deprived of all their rights'. He was also struck by the ill-treatment of the island's Indigenous population. Soon after arriving he saw an old Nivkh man being harangued by the children of the bathhouse owner. 'Some day I will study them,' he wrote in his diary. Even for a writer as inquisitive as Chekhov, the Indigenous population of northern Sakhalin was little more than an incomprehensible shadow at the edge of his field of vision. The Nivkh, the largest Indigenous group on the island today, are one of the five Indigenous peoples of eastern Siberia known by ethnologists as 'Palaeo-Asiatics', whose languages have no known connection with other linguistic groups. (Nivkh, famously, has twenty-six different ways of counting from one to ten according to the physical and social characteristics of the thing being counted.) Traditionally they were semi-nomadic fishers, with an animist belief system based around four 'spirit masters': the sky, the hills, water and fire. Today most Nivkh live on the other side of the island, in the oil towns of the north-east, having been displaced from their traditional settlements under Soviet collectivisation.

'Nothing is sadder than a boat on land,' said Natalia, gazing through a gap in the hoardings surrounding the harbour. Pining for the past was a form of self-comfort, and near ubiquitous among those I spoke to on Sakhalin. It was also a way of explaining the corrupt and diffuse present to strangers. Things haven't always been this way. When she was a child, she told me, the town had 20,000 people and nine schools; today the population is half that and there are three schools. At least in Chekhov's day the place had a purpose. Now, said Natalia, the young people fled to Yuzhho-Sakhalinsk, Moscow or Vladivostok the moment they left school.

On the outskirts of the town, as in the villages I would see over the coming days, occupied houses were often surrounded by dozens of rotting dwellings shrouded in weeds, home only to feral dogs and the occasional bear. Natalia remembered the sunny days of Young

Pioneer camps in the hills; the days when the port was thriving and she and her school friends would return from summer afternoons on the beach glittering with black dust from the coal barges.

Now the coal industry was defunct and the timber firms had moved to Japan. Alexandrovsk, like much of the island, saw little of the vast wealth being siphoned from the oil and gas fields of the north-east (the largest consortium, Sakhalin Energy, reported revenue of over $6 billion in 2018, but most of the tax was skimmed off by Moscow). There were no longer enough fish in the Tatar Strait to sustain the town's fishing industry, and the water had risen to permanently submerge her childhood beach. Who knew why? She didn't want to reconcile herself to this present – it was not her country.

A hundred yards offshore, crowned white with bird droppings, was the trio of sandstone outcrops known as the Three Brothers. Half a mile south, on a hillside above the shore, stood a derelict lighthouse, which had recently been requisitioned by the army for some unspecified purpose and therefore could not be visited, I was warned, or even approached. High above the ruins, on the top of the hill, was the site of the old lighthouse – 'a modest little cottage with a mast and lamp' – to which Chekhov made regular walks during his months in Alexandrovsk. (There was nothing there now but the concrete footings of a dismantled radio mast.) Chekhov would not stoop to presenting a lighthouse as a symbol of anything, least of all hope, but its setting did promise a kind of transcendence:

> The higher one rises, the more freely one breathes; the sea stretches out before one's eyes, and little by little thoughts arise which have nothing to do with prison, or hard labour, or the penal colony, and it is only up here that one becomes aware of how wearisome and hard life is down below. Day in, day out, the hard-labourers and settled exiles undergo their punishment, while, from morning to evening, those at liberty talk only about who has been flogged, who has tried to run off, who has

been recaptured and who is going to be flogged; and it's strange how you yourself become accustomed to these conversations . . . But on the mountain, in sight of the sea and the beautiful ravines, all this comes to seem impossibly cheap and sordid, as in truth it really is.

Beyond the old landing stage the Tatar Strait was without a hint of colour. As Natalia and I approached the gates to the harbour, two dogs emerged barking from a watchman's concrete hut. I sized them up, declared them 'fine', and turned around to photograph the plaque commemorating Chekhov's arrival.

8

Natalia had met Miromanov, the museum director, forty years ago, when they were trainee teachers at a Young Pioneer camp. She spoke of him as if he were famous – which he was, in a limited sense. She didn't think he would remember her. 'He did something very special. It was really remarkable. He would say, "Tell me any word, and I will make a poem." And he did just that: you gave him a word and immediately, he would recite a perfect rhyming verse; I don't mean doggerel.'

Miromanov was shaven-headed and grey-bearded, with the complexion of a fisherman. He was impatient with anyone who was not a young woman. He'd been born in Alexandrovsk, like Natalia, and for a while had been mayor. Before that he had travelled the world. When I asked in what capacity, he changed the subject with such deftness that I only realised he had done so hours later. He was popular, and the way others addressed him, with a cautious smile, suggested he still wielded the power of a person known to be influential. I asked him many questions and not once did he ponder his answer for more than a second, even when it was a snapped 'I do not *know!*' You wouldn't take him for a museum director or, for that matter, darling of the town's am-dram soc. (People swooned over his Vanya.)

The Chekhov Museum, located in a traditional wooden house built on the spot where the author stayed, had been run by Miromanov's father before him: the next day he showed me in with the manner of someone presenting the family business to an investor. The rooms were immaculate, the letters and artefacts (Anton Pavlovich's desk; Anton Pavlovich's samovar . . .) displayed with none of the pathos – blown light bulbs, Blu-Tacked labelling, lurking cats – of some Russian regional museums. A cleaner followed us from room to room, wiping the vitrines like the cleaners who glide from icon to icon in Orthodox churches, cleaning lip-smears from the glass.

Soon after he arrived, Chekhov arranged for 10,000 census forms to be printed – 'my main aim in conducting the census was not its results but the impressions received during the making of it'. These forms, a remarkable 5,000 of which were completed, formed the basis for the book he would publish three years later. The forms included lines for birthplace, year of arrival, literacy level and family circumstances, as well as 'status' – whether the subject was free, a 'settled exile', a 'peasant-in-exile' or a convict.

At the time of Chekhov's visit, Miromanov said, Sakhalin had four categories of convict. Most slept in the town's prison, were not shackled and worked each day in the coal mines at Dué ('a dreadful, hideous place', according to Chekhov, which lay on the coast beyond the lighthouse). A second group was shackled and laboured for four hours per day. The third and most wretched were the *tachechniki*, who were chained for life to wooden wheelbarrows. The *tachechniki* did not work but sat or lay in their cell, the barrow serving only as ball-and-chain. (There were photos of these men standing with their barrows, wearing the expression of those who have discovered that pain is not a finite thing, an expression that might be a sarcastic imitation of one in rapture.) Finally there was a small number of political exiles, numbering no more than fifty at the time of Chekhov's visit, including *narodniki* like Lev Shternberg.

9

The dog bite, once the swelling subsided, seemed to kindle a yearning to move. I had read about a village to the north of Alexandrovsk, which had been designated as a kind of exile within exile. In 1890, when the authorities in Alexandrovsk learned about the approach of the famous author, clutching his wretched notepad, they saw to it that one political exile, a tiresome agitator for prisoners' rights, would not be around to blab. Shternberg had been in Alexandrovsk for more than a year, and had become sickened by the ill-treatment of the convicts he lived among, especially the overseers' often arbitrary meting out of punishment beatings. One of the most memorable scenes in Chekhov's *Sakhalin Island* describes the birch-lashing of a failed escapee, a child-killer named Prokhorov:

> Prokhorov's hair is stuck to his brow, his neck is swollen; after five or ten blows his body, still covered by weals from previous lashings, has already turned crimson and dark blue; the skin on it splits from every blow. 'Yer Excellency!' we hear through the screeching and weeping. 'Yer excellency! Be merciful, yer Excellency!'

Chekhov notes a 'kind of curious stretching-out of the neck, the sound of retching'. He leaves, unable to watch any more.

Writing a few years later, another visitor, Charles Hawes, describes the *plet*, a whip with lead-tipped thongs. Hawes tells the story of one victim who, sentenced to a hundred strokes, promised to pay the executioner with a bottle of vodka (then a rare commodity) if he refrained from applying the leaded tips. But with five strokes remaining, the prisoner reneged: 'You can't hurt me now; you needn't think you'll get your vodka!' The executioner silently adjusted his stroke. Three more blows and the man was dead. 'It was only necessary to draw back the *plet*, as the stroke was spent,' explains Hawes, 'for the ends to injure the liver and send a clot of blood to the heart.'

In 1890, shortly before Chekhov's arrival, Shternberg was induced to sign an agreement promising to cease his complaints about such treatment, on pain of being banished to the 'most isolated corner of Sakhalin'. Having persisted, he was expelled to a tiny settlement fifty miles north. Chekhov had little to say about Viakhtu, noting only that salmon and sturgeon were caught in the nearby estuary. If Alexandrovsk was the 'world's end' then Viakhtu was a space station. Miromanov said there was 'nothing to see' there, but he agreed to take me, as long as the road had not been washed away, and as long as I paid for fuel and vodka.

10

At 5 a.m. a dented red Land Cruiser pulled into Alexandrovsk's main square. Before he introduced me to the man in the back, Miromanov introduced me to Suzanne, who was the car.

'It is very important to name your vehicle.' He patted the dashboard. 'I knew she was called Suzanne as soon as I drove her.'

The man in the back was his friend Vladimir, the museum's manager. He seldom spoke, but sang all the way to Viakhtu, and doled out the vodka. Both he and Miromanov had dressed in camouflage fishing overalls, in the trunk were their waders and tackle, and next to Vladimir was enough vodka to make the Red Army Choir botch its cue. They couldn't have cared less about Shternberg.

I had looked up Viakhtu in an atlas of Sakhalin, but the modern village was not Shternberg's. His was what Miromanov called 'Old Viakhtu', a mile north on the other side of an estuary, accessible only by boat. And there, on the map, I saw it: Shternberg's 'Russian Palestine', a featureless plain locked between forest and water, labelled *Nezhil*, short for 'uninhabited'.

It was the phase of insupportable wetness between winter and summer, when the earth is released from snow only to find itself flooded. The dead grass had the flattened look of hair that has been under a hat all day. The hares that crossed our path – a sign of bad luck, said Miromanov – were still shucking off their white winter coat. To cross the sagging wooden bridges felt like an act of fatalism. The road rolled through fishing villages whose names I knew from Chekhov: Mgachi, Tangi, Khoe, Trambaus. I was aware it was an unrepresentative time of year, transitional. Everything was a snow-dozed entropic mess, and the light was too flat to shake it into beauty.

Miromanov knew the name of none of the plants – 'I do not *know*!' – and was coldly unmoved by a sunrise that caused me to twist in my seat for a better look. His relationship with the natural world was more visceral. 'I have been all around the world. Really, everywhere is the same – Russia, Scotland, America . . . But I could not live in any country where you must release a fish when you have caught it. Why? *Why?*' He made a gun of his fingers and shot himself under the chin with a great woof of laughter.

At a fork in the road, we stopped and Vladimir divvied vodka into tin cups, and each of us opened our door and tipped the contents onto the road – libation, he said, to the Nivkh god Bordh, whose domain began there. Vladimir refilled the cups and Englishly I proffered a toast to Sakhalin (spirits make me expansive).

'No!' Miromanov spat. 'Sak-ha-lin! The – hole – of – the – *arse*.'

Another cosmology.

11

Viakhtu – 'New Viakhtu' – was situated on the edge of a bank of dunes, a cluster of brightly painted timber houses around a rutted crossroads. Outside his smallholding we met Obet, the fisherman who would ferry us across the estuary to Old Viakhtu.

Obet's camp on the sand peninsula opposite Old Viakhtu was a breaker's yard of engine blocks and ship's doors. An old orange bus was used as shelter, its window frames caulked with expanding foam against draughts. Welded to its undercarriage, in place of wheels, were sledge-runners made of scrolled iron drainage pipe. While we waited for the tide, I dozed inside and watched Miromanov and Vladimir casting their lines into the race.

After two hours the tide turned and Obet deemed the water deep enough. Miromanov donned a long oiled cape. The sea was violent and very cold, swimming with submerged tree trunks and branches; only afterwards, back at the camp, did I understand that it was not a journey Obet would have risked in such a small boat had I not been paying, and that the laughter of Vladimir and Miromanov had been nervous laughter. Fifteen minutes later, sodden and breathless, we pulled the boat onto a beach and climbed a low sandy cliff to the headland.

'Nothing!' said Miromanov, looking around.

Well, next to nothing: the raised outlines of foundations cloaked by tall dead grass; the smothered mouth of a well; a few timbers; patches of whortleberries, stunted spruce, a species of thornbush coming into bud . . . But otherwise only the dark edge of the woods bounding the plain to the north and the tarnished estuary we'd crossed to the south. A 'lonely, abandoned grave in the empty taiga', Shternberg called it.

As well as five houses occupied by freed convicts, a small company of soldiers had been based here, since it was a known crossing point for escaped convicts bound for Cape Pogibi. The peninsula was also, as it had been for thousands of years, a way station for semi-nomadic Nivkh. The end of the world, then, but the beginning of another. For Shternberg it was the site of his 'ethnographic baptism'. Did he remember the advice his mother gave him, as he boarded the *Petersburg* back in Odessa? 'You are a kind person, and God is just, and He exists everywhere, even on Sakhalin. He will not abandon you.'

He had only a screened corner of the soldiers' cabin, but somehow he made a kind of home. On the wall were photos of his friends; he practised calisthenics, chopped wood, worked on his English. He read – Dante (of course) and Max Weber's *The Agrarian Sociology of Ancient Civilizations*. Most importantly, he was 'frequently visited by the sons of the taiga'. Despite his lack of any training, his research into the kinship and spiritual traditions of the Nivkh established him as a major figure in the emergent field of Russian ethnography, a discipline to which he would devote the rest of his life. During the remainder of his sentence, the authorities in Alexandrovsk, who had a strategic interest in monitoring the 'natives', allowed him to mount several expeditions to Nivkh settlements in the island's north and even to the Amur delta. His 1905 monograph on *The Social Organisation of the Gilyak* (as the Nivkh were then known) is considered a classic, and his description of Nivkh 'group marriage' was eagerly championed by Friedrich Engels as supporting his and Marx's evolutionist theory of class struggle.

'His idealism, so full of enthusiasm, became even deeper,' wrote a friend on meeting the freed exile (he returned to Zhitomir, under police surveillance, in 1898). 'His rich imagination became even richer, and his faith in humankind and its bright future even more passionate than before.' Nor were his religious or political convictions subdued. In 1907 he became director of St Petersburg's Jewish Museum, and as late as 1921 the venerated ethnographer, aged sixty, was arrested and briefly imprisoned as a socialist agitator.

Back at the fishing camp Vladimir built a fire in the lee of the bus and hung a pot of water over it from a crook of driftwood. He added potatoes, dill, the salmon he had caught, salt, lemon juice, vodka. We sat in the bus and ate and drank. My bandage was soaked and my leg throbbed, but not unpleasantly. Back at home a week later I'd be prescribed an emergency course of rabies jabs – the one I'd had, it turned out, was for tetanus.

12

' God's world is good,' Chekhov told Aleksey Suvorin when he got home to Moscow. 'The only thing that is not good is us.'

The memory of those few weeks in 1890 became a kind of treasured wound to him. Towards the end of his life, Miromanov told me, self-exiled in Yalta for his health, Chekhov was asked why he had always been reluctant to talk about his time on Sakhalin. He paced up and down, as was his habit, and went to a window. Finally he said,

'Afterwards, everything was Sakhalinised, through and through . . .'

He might have meant his country, the prison state it had become by 1904; but I think it more likely he was referring to the spirit of exile with which those two dark months had infected him, his sense that he had never truly come home.

Over the following days I received a series of text messages from my father. They contained no words, just emojis of flags, black flags. I thought of Shternberg's anarchism, and of the 'dark flag' under which the *Petersburg* was said to sail. When I replied – 'Everything okay?' – I would receive no answer, until, the next night, in my train bunk or rehydrating noodles in some seedy hotel, I received another of those chilling semaphores from 5,000 miles away:

I took the flags as a symbol less of grief, let alone rebellion, than of negation. But it turned out that was a misreading, for those messages, from deep in the hold, marked the start of my father's navigating a course back to the world.

13

Towards the end of May I took a train to the oil town of Nogliki, in the north-east, about 75 miles from Alexandrovsk-Sakhalinsky. If 'oil town' makes it sound booming it was not – merely a place where the offshore platforms were the main employer. From the bridge overlooking the Tym River the water was a stew of timber, whole tree trunks turning slowly in the current. The body of the river was ochre with sediment washed off the mountains; but a tributary was leaking into it the black water of the bogs. And the black was somehow cleaner than the ochre, the black of an eye's pupil. I was reminded of something Natalia had told me, that the old Japanese name for Sakhalin translated as 'the Island of the Black River'.

Nearby, on a lagoon, two young Nivkh men were feeding a bonfire with sheets of damp plywood. Warming herself by the fire, though it wasn't cold, was their mother, Angela. She was fifty and wore a bright yellow Puffa jacket and large blue-framed glasses. Her family had been living in this quiet corner of the world, ten miles from Nogliki, for as long as the world has existed – before collectivisation, before colonisation. The clearing contained a large single-storey timber house, patched with sheets of wood, and adjoining sheds for firewood and fishing tackle. A track sloped through the retarded larches typical of this thin soil, to a seaweed-strewn beach cluttered with upturned wooden boats and nets beyond mending. On the horizon, like a contrail, was the mile-long spit that sheltered the lagoon from the violence of the Sea of Okhotsk and made it a sanctuary for salmon.

'If there is no fish there is no life,' said Angela. 'You catch fish or you get ill. For our people it is a genetic need.'

I'd stopped here by chance but it was as if she had been expecting me. She was unsurprised by my questions, incurious. The bonfire smoke plumed and dissipated scentlessly. The peacefulness was that of a very old place settling still deeper into itself. There was no phone signal, no gas, no power.

During the purges of the 1930s as many as a third of all Nivkh men on the island were killed by the NKVD (precursor of the KGB and today's FSB), usually on suspicion of spying for Japan. Under the USSR, the Nivkh were subjected to two phases of resettlement: first, in the 1930s, collectivisation into kolkhozes, then, in the 1960s, *ukrupneniye*, or 'centralisation' – the concentration of the kolkhozes into yet larger agricultural centres, such as Nogliki. The effect of these mandatory relocations has been to depopulate huge swathes of land. Of more than 1,000 traditional settlements scattered along the northern coast in 1962, by 1986 there were only 329. Angela's was one of the rare families to have returned to land it occupied before collectivisation.

She herself was a poet, and we talked about the famous Nivkh writer Vladimir Sangi, master of the language and its stories, and champion of the Nivkh alphabet. He lived in Nogliki but he was ailing, too old for meetings with strange Englishmen.

On the fingers of one hand Angela counted off the speakers of Nivkh she knew, all of them women.

'The only man who speaks the language is Sangi,' she said. 'We can dance like real Nivkh, we can sing and fish like real Nivkh, we can make clothes like real Nivkh. But the language we have lost, and a nation without a language is not a nation.'

The quiet of the lagoon was enlarged by a sandpiper's flight call. In turn its flurry of stifled peeps was made to sound bleak by the vastness of the setting. Between the two, between the lagoon and the bird, there seemed to unfold a space of infinite hospitality.

Angela said, 'We have a house in Nogliki, but genetically we cannot live there. It's better to stay here, where it's cold. This is our place.' ∎

CONTRIBUTORS

Alison Anderson has translated nearly a hundred novels from French, including works by Amélie Nothomb, J.M.G. Le Clézio, Muriel Barbery and Laurent Gaudé.

Katherine Angel is the author of *Unmastered: A Book on Desire, Most Difficult to Tell* and *Tomorrow Sex Will Be Good Again*, forthcoming from Verso in 2021. She teaches creative and critical writing at Birkbeck, University of London.

William Atkins is the author of *The Immeasurable World: A Desert Journey*, which was awarded the 2019 Stanford Dolman Travel Book of the Year. He is guest-editing a forthcoming issue of *Granta* devoted to travel writing.

Tash Aw is the author of four critically acclaimed novels, which have won the Whitbread First Novel Award, a regional Commonwealth Writers' Prize and twice been longlisted for the Man Booker Prize. He is also the author of the memoir *The Face: Strangers on a Pier*, which was a finalist for the *Los Angeles Times* Book Prize. He was recently the Judith Ginsberg Fellow at the Columbia Institute of Ideas and Imagination in Paris. His latest novel, *We, The Survivors*, was published this year.

Ken Babstock is the author of five collections of poetry, most recently *On Malice*. His collection *Methodist Hatchet* won the 2012 Griffin Poetry Prize. He lives in Toronto with his son.

Guillermo Bleichmar teaches at St John's College in Santa Fe, New Mexico. In addition to translating Antonio Muñoz Molina, he is the editor and translator of *Country of Bullets: Chronicles of War* by Colombian journalist Juanita León and Johannes Kepler's *The Six-Cornered Snowflake*.

Melitta Breznik was born in Austria in 1961. After working as a general practitioner and psychiatrist, her writing career began in 1995 with *Nachdienst*, which has been translated into several languages.

Nicola Lo Calzo is an Italian photographer. His books include *Regla, Obia* and *Inside Niger*, and he is a regular contributor to *Le Monde*, the *New Yorker*, the *Wall Street Journal*, the *New York Times* and *Internazionale*.

Anne Carson was born in Canada and works in Iceland. 'Visitors Rev. 4' was inspired by Ragnar Kjartansson's haunted installation *The Visitors*.

Charlotte Collins is a literary translator from German and co-chair of the UK Translators Association. Her translation of Robert Seethaler's *A Whole Life* was shortlisted for the 2016 Man Booker International Prize. Her co-translation, with Ruth Martin, of *The Eighth Life* by Nino Haratischvili will be published by Scribe UK in November 2019.

Linda Coverdale has translated over eighty books, including works by Marguerite Duras, Tahar Ben Jelloun, Roland Barthes and Marie Darrieussecq. A Chevalier de l'Ordre des Arts et des Lettres, she has won the 2006 Scott Moncrieff Prize, the MLA Aldo & Jeanne Scaglione Literary Translation Prize and the 2004 International IMPAC Dublin Literary Award.

Marie Darrieussecq is the author of over twenty books, including novels, essays, a play, a biography and translations. In 2013 she was awarded the Prix Médicis and the Prix des Prix for her novel *Il faut beaucoup aimer les hommes*.

Lara Feigel is the author of four books, including *The Love-charm of Bombs*, *The Bitter Taste of Victory* and, most recently, *Free Woman: Life, Liberation and Doris Lessing*. She is a Fellow of the Royal Society of Literature.

Bruno Fert is a French photographer whose work has won the Académie des Beaux-Arts Award, the Neuflize Collection Award and the Roger Pic Award. His book *Refuge* will be published by Autrement in November 2019.

Polly Gannon holds a PhD in Russian literature from Cornell University and is past Director of Cultural Studies at the New York-St Petersburg Institute of Linguistics, Cognition and Culture.

Laurent Gaudé is a French novelist and playwright. His novel *The House of Scorta* won the 2004 Prix Goncourt, and his most recent novel is *Hear Our Defeats*.

Alicja Gescinska is an award-winning Belgian-Polish novelist and philosopher. From 2016 to 2017 she presented *Wanderlust*, a philosophical programme for the Flemish public broadcaster.

Peter Graves is an Honorary Fellow of Scandinavian Studies at the University of Edinburgh, where he taught for many years.

Romesh Gunesekera's first novel *Reef* was published twenty-five years ago. His latest novel is *Suncatcher*.

Colin Herd is a poet and lecturer at the University of Glasgow. His previous collections include *Too Ok*, *Glovebox* and *Click & Collect*. A new collection, *You Name It*, is forthcoming from Dostoevsky Wannabe.

Michael Hofmann is the translator of more than seventy books from the German, including works by Franz Kafka, Hans Fallada, Joseph Roth, Gottfried Benn and Peter Stamm. Hofmann's most recent collection of poems is *One Lark, One Horse*.

Srećko Horvat is a philosopher and the author of a dozen books, most recently *Poetry from the Future: Why a Global Liberation Movement Is Our Civilisation's Last Chance*.

Joseph Leo Koerner is a Professor of History of Art at Harvard University. His most recent book is *Bosch and Bruegel: From Enemy Painting to Everyday Life*. His film *The Burning Child* was released in 2019.

Daisy Lafarge lives in Glasgow. A collection of poetry and a novel, *Paul*, are forthcoming with Granta Books.

Nam Le is the author of *The Boat*. He lives in Melbourne, Australia.

Tom McCarthy is a novelist whose work has been translated into more than twenty languages. His first novel, *Remainder*, won the 2008 Believer Book Award and has been adapted for cinema, theatre and radio. His third, *C*, was a 2010 Booker Prize finalist, as was his fourth, *Satin Island*, in 2015. He is currently a Guest Professor at Stadelschule Frankfurt and Fellow of the DAAD Artists-in-Berlin Programme.

Andrew Miller is the author of eight novels including *Ingenious Pain*, winner of the 1999 International IMPAC Dublin Literary Award, and *Pure*, winner of the 2012 Costa Book of the Year. His most recent novel is *Now We Shall Be Entirely Free*.

Caroline Albertine Minor is the author of the novel *Pura vida* and the short-story collection *Blessings*, which was awarded the 2017 Michael Strunge Prize and the 2018 P.O. Enquist Prize.

Peter Mishler's debut collection of poetry is *Fludde*. New poems are forthcoming in the *American Poetry Review*.

Antonio Muñoz Molina is the author of more than thirty books. His novel *Like a Fading Shadow* was shortlisted for the 2018 Man

Booker International Prize. 'Office of Lost Moments' is an excerpt from *To Walk Alone in the Crowd*, forthcoming from Farrar, Straus & Giroux in the USA and Serpent's Tail in the UK.

Ulf Karl Olov Nilsson, also known as UKON, is a poet and a psychoanalyst working in Gothenburg, Sweden. He has published fifteen collections of poetry and a book of essays, *Glömskans bibliotek* (The Library of Oblivion).

Ekin Oklap translates from Turkish and Italian. She was shortlisted for the 2016 Man Booker International Prize for her translation of *A Strangeness in My Mind* by Orhan Pamuk.

Orhan Pamuk, the 2006 laureate of the Nobel Prize in Literature, is the author of ten novels and the memoir *Istanbul*. One of Europe's most prominent novelists, his work has been translated into over sixty languages.

Jacqueline Rose is the author of more than ten books. A regular contributor to the *London Review of Books*, she is a co-founder of Independent Jewish Voices in the UK and a Fellow of the British Academy.

Elif Shafak's most recent book, *10 Minutes 38 Seconds in this Strange World*, has been shortlisted for the 2019 Booker Prize. Shafak is a Chevalier de l'Ordre des Arts et des Lettres and is a Fellow of the Royal Society of Literature.

Ludmila Ulitskaya is the author of fifteen works of fiction, three tales for children and six plays. In 2001 she won the Russian Booker Prize and in 2013 was made an Officier de la Légion d'honneur by the French government.

Caroline Waight is an award-winning literary translator working from Danish and German. Recent publications include *The Invention of Ana*, *The Chestnut Man* and *The Gravediggers*, forthcoming from Profile in 2020.

Adam Weymouth is a journalist. His first book, *The Kings of the Yukon: A River Journey in Search of the Chinook*, won the 2018 Sunday Times / Peters Fraser + Dunlop Young Writer of the Year Award and the 2019 Lonely Planet Adventure Travel Book of the Year. He is currently living in Lesbos.